W9-BGR-746

START YOUR BUSINESS

A Beginner's Guide

Compiled and Edited by
Vickie Reierson

OASIS PRESS

The Oasis Press® / PSI Research
Grants Pass, Oregon

072095

Published by The Oasis Press®/PSI Research

This publication is designed to provide accurate and authoritative information in regard to the subject matter covered. It is sold with the understanding that the publisher is not engaged in rendering legal, accounting, or other professional service. If legal advice or other expert assistance is required, the services of a competent professional person should be sought.

> *— from a declaration of principles jointly adopted by a committee of the American Bar Association and a committee of publishers.*

Managing Editor: Vickie Reierson
Assistant Editor: Linda Pinkham
Typographers: C. C. Dickinson & Melanie Whalon
Cover and graphics designer: Studio Silicon

Please direct any comments, questions, or suggestions regarding this book to The Oasis Press®/ PSI Research:

> Editorial Department
> 300 North Valley Drive
> Grants Pass, OR 97526
> (503) 479-9464
> (800) 228-2275

The Oasis Press® is a Registered Trademark of Publishing Services, Inc., an Oregon corporation doing business as PSI Research.

Library of Congress Cataloging-in-Publication Data
Start your business : a beginner's guide / compiled and edited by
  Vickie Reierson. -- 2nd ed.
      p. cm. -- (PSI successful business library)
  Includes index.
  ISBN 1-55571-363-7 (pbk.)
  1. New business enterprises--United States--Handbooks, manuals,
etc.   I. Reierson, Vickie.   II. Series.
HD62.5.S737 1995   95-532
658.1'141--dc20   CIP

Printed in the United States of America
Second edition 10 9 8 7 6 5 4 3 2 1 0

 Printed on recycled paper when available.

Table of Contents

Preface

Since its publication in the fall of 1993, not only has *Start Your Business* proven to be a helpful, organizational resource for thousands of beginning entrepreneurs, it has also received national recognition as a quality, start-up business book. In its April 1994 issue, *Inc.* magazine selected the book as one of its Top 40 Start-Up Business Books for beginning entrepreneurs. Because of the book's favorable reception in the marketplace, and The Oasis Press' ongoing commitment to providing accurate and up-to-date business information to small business owners, the editors and authors of The Oasis Press decided to do a thorough review and update of the text.

As a result of this effort, the second edition of *Start Your Business* features several new sections of informative text, new and updated checklists on a variety of business topics, and additional helpful resource listings. Some of the highlights include:

- New checklists in Chapter 2 on business insurance, credit policies, writing a financing proposal, financial management, and tax-saving tips;

- A new section in Chapter 3 on how to do market research;

- A completely new section in Chapter 8 on how to buy an existing business; and

- A new Appendix C, which features a listing of national and state-specific business magazines.

Now, more than ever, *Start Your Business* is a timely, up-to-date book that will make playing the business game easier. Take control of your business' future by empowering yourself with solid business information and a sound plan of action before opening your doors.

Here at The Oasis Press, we wish you the very best in your business endeavors and goals; we applaud your drive and enthusiasm. With knowledge and preplanning, you will only succeed in making your business concept a profitable reality.

Vickie Reierson, Editor
The Oasis Press/PSI Research
July 1995

Preface to First Edition

For more than a decade, the goal of every Oasis Press business book has been to provide practical, hands-on information in such a way that budding entrepreneurs or existing business owners could easily understand and apply the information to everyday business operations, and use it to help ensure their success. Because of this goal, we, the editors at The Oasis Press, have dedicated ourselves to:

- Researching various business topics and issues as thoroughly and accurately as possible;
- Rewriting technical legalese or formal business writing into easy-to-read, layperson text; and
- Designing pages and books for ease of use and clarity.

The books we have helped produce over the years have a wide range of topics. For instance, The Successful Business Library, which boasts more than 30 titles, contains books on accounting, marketing, franchising, mail order, business environmental concerns, business plan writing, and personnel management, to name a few. In addition, the *Starting and Operating a Business in ...* series, which features a book for each state, plus the District of Columbia, provides updated, state-specific and federal business information that is crucial for anyone in business.

At a recent editorial meeting, where we were discussing new book ideas for The Successful Business Library, we realized that none of our books — nor any of the ones we have encountered in our past research — have specifically dealt with providing a general list of what a future business owner will need to do, be required to do, or should consider doing before opening his or her business. It seemed all this information was available in various books, but not under one convenient cover. We thought about the thousands of people out there who wanted to start a business, but were looking for an all-in-one book that would simply list all the major requirements and issues a new business owner needs to know, without going into all the details.

So after some excited talk and brainstorming, we decided to help those people and produce a basic, quick-read book that would highlight all the major areas of starting a business by listing, in a check-off format, all the to-dos for starting a business. This information was readily available to us through all our current book titles, our expert authors, and other in-house business resources. We just needed to research, compile, and organize this information into one handy format and easy-to-read text.

Start Your Business is the result of that initial editorial meeting and subsequent research. This book is for anyone who wants to start a business, who isn't sure about what it all entails, and who wants a brief overview of what is and can be involved in starting a business. Make no bones about it — building up a business is a lot of work and can seem daunting at times. Because of this, we tried to give the book an air of festivity and ease with the business game motif; general, short introductions; and convenient check-off boxes to note what business owners need to do or may want to do before opening their doors.

As comprehensive as our research was, we by no means want to imply this book covers every detail of start up for every type of business. Rather, it is a general guide, or if you will, rule book, for the beginner to get him or her to understand the business game better, and to encourage that individual to make the first move to starting a successful business. By knowing what to expect, the beginning business player will be better prepared, more knowledgeable, and more likely to win.

Vickie Reierson, Editor
The Oasis Press/PSI Research
October 1993

How to Use this Book

Start Your Business was created to help a beginning business owner or entrepreneur feel more confident about starting a business by providing general checklists on all the activities and requirements involved in doing so.

As a prospective business owner, you may be pleased with this book's intent, but you may still feel overwhelmed by the idea of starting a business simply because of the numerous checklists you may have seen while leafing through the book.

How to Approach the Text

First of all, don't be intimidated! The eight topics discussed in this book may not all apply to your particular business. So before you get discouraged, simply look through the Table of Contents, or review the list below, and see which topics apply to your business concept or idea.

- Chapter 1 discusses the legal requirements that are necessary for starting a business. You can also get ideas and tips about where to locate your business and how to set up your office.
- Chapter 2 helps you decide whether you need sources of funding and where to look for funding. It also features handy checklists on business insurance and financial management issues.
- Chapter 3 highlights the importance of strategizing and planning your marketing activities before opening your doors.

From activities on how to conduct research to planning a media mix, you will learn marketing basics at a glance.

- Chapter 4 informs you about all the activities and requirements that come into the picture once you hire an employee. This chapter emphasizes staffing procedures, government regulations for employers, and personnel paperwork.

- Chapter 5 is about producing your product or service, and it provides information on overall issues regarding production, warehousing and shipping, and inventory.

- Chapter 6 deals with a hot topic: environmental concerns and laws. Find out what environmental laws apply to your business and what activities you will need to complete. In addition, learn about ways to save money and help the environment at the same time.

- Chapter 7 takes you through the process of developing a business plan. You may not have to do a business plan initially, but it is a good idea to think about doing one anyway. Business plans are a great way for you to investigate your business and be knowledgeable about its financial needs, marketing strategies, long-term goals, and operations.

- Chapter 8 concludes the book with a discussion on buying a business or franchise. This option may or may not apply to you; however, if you decide to buy a business or franchise, this chapter is a good reference and starting point.

So, if you are going to start your own service company out of your house and operate as a sole proprietorship, you will not be concerned with Chapter 4 on employees or Chapter 8 on buying a business or franchise. You may not even be interested in doing a business plan (Chapter 7). The number of applicable topics you will have to deal with will vary depending on your particular situation.

Once you have determined which chapters you are interested in reviewing, first read through the chapters in their entirety. Don't stop to check off activities or make notes. Use your first read-through to familiarize yourself with the content and checklists, and to look up any unfamiliar terms in Appendix A. After your initial review is finished for each chapter, decide which chapter you need to concentrate on first, second, and so forth.

When you are ready to begin with your first chapter, be prepared to check off activities and write notes to yourself on the side. You will note the book occasionally provides you with blank lines for listing certain items. Feel free to jot down any notes on these lines.

As you read along, check off any activities that are required for your business and any activities that may prove helpful. You will notice many of the activities listed throughout *Start Your Business* are not necessarily legal requirements, rather they are suggested options and precautions so you will avoid making costly mistakes and be more prepared as a business owner.

Carefully evaluate each activity to see if it is something you feel you should do. If you have trouble understanding an activity, highlight it or mark it some way so you can come back to it later. Often, reading further in the text will help clarify these activities.

Helpful Resources

If you still have trouble understanding an activity or particular group of activities, refer to the Helpful Resources section, which is featured at the end of each chapter. This section provides you with additional resources for finding out more information regarding the topic area discussed in a chapter.

Remember, *Start Your Business* is a summary of several major business topics, and every detail cannot be covered. As a result, the Helpful Resources section was created to help you locate more information and materials.

Many of the resources listed in the Helpful Resources are Oasis Press business books, government agencies, national associations, and on-line information services. Some of the information in several of the chapters is drawn heavily from current Oasis Press books. The Oasis Press' business books are good sources of information, and they are readily available through bookstores. Nothing is more frustrating than to refer a person to a book or resource and find it is no longer in print, not published yet, or on back order. Consequently, all the resources listed in this edition, including all Oasis Press books, have been verified as available.

So, if you want to get more details on a particular subject, first look at the First Aid section, which immediately follows every chapter's introduction, to see which book is the best source for more information. Then, if you are interested in other aspects of the chapter's topics, check out the Helpful Resources section.

Plan of Action Worksheets

Once you have finished reviewing all the checklists in a chapter, and you have marked off those activities you want to do, you are ready for the Plan of Action worksheets located at the end of every chapter. These worksheets are designed as an organizing and tracking tool for the checked-off activities in the chapter.

How to use the worksheets is mainly up to you. The basic premise of the worksheets is to provide a convenient place for you to organize, prioritize, and track the necessary activities. The worksheets provide columns for you to indicate what action needs to be taken, when it should be started, who will be responsible for carrying it out, and what the deadline is for each activity.

If you feel there are too many checked-off activities in the chapter to list all at once on the worksheets, start off with just a few of the activities that seem most pertinent and time consuming. Pick the top 25, for example, and list them in the order of priority you feel they should be completed. When you have prioritized and organized these activities, you can pick the next 25 and go from there.

Another strategy may be to list all the activities you have marked off in the chapter under the "Action to be Taken" column on the worksheets. Then, using highlighters, go back and highlight (in a particular color) all the activities that need to be done first. Pick another highlighter color for all the activities you want to do next, and so on. Once you are done prioritizing, you can go back and determine who will do what, and when.

Another strategy for completing the Plan of Action worksheets is to do them on your computer using this book's companion software which is discussed on the following page.

Regardless of the method you will employ for organizing and tracking your activities, be sure to cut out each Plan of Action worksheet so you can make several copies. You most likely will need several copies for each chapter.

When you have done the Plan of Action worksheets for each of the appropriate chapters, you will have a good handle on what it will take to start your business. These Plan of Action worksheets will prove quite valuable in getting you into the business game in better shape. You will have a game plan and sense of what it is going to take to win!

Companion Software

If you have an IBM/PC computer with Windows™, you can do your Plan of Action worksheets on-screen, using *Start Your Business Software*. This companion software follows each of the checklists in this book and helps you create your plan of action for each topic you need to consider. To help you get a better idea of how the program complements the book, here is an illustration of the program's input screen.

With *Start Your Business Software,* you can easily indicate:

- If you want to complete a particular action,
- Who will be responsible,
- When it needs to be done, and
- Any notes you want to include.

Once you have identified the actions you need to do, the software allows you to sort the actions in a variety of ways. For instance, you can organize your activities by deadline, responsible person, or a mix of both. In addition, you can print out a customized Plan of Action worksheet for each person responsible for helping you with your business preplanning.

This software is a great time-saver and will help streamline your preplanning experience. If you are interested in learning more about *Start Your Business Software*, please contact the Sales Department at The Oasis Press/PSI Research.

Appendices

This edition of *Start Your Business* features three appendices:

- Appendix A provides many business term definitions that will hopefully clarify some of the activities in the chapters, plus prove to be educational for some.

- Appendix B is a current listing of all the state director offices for the Small Business Development Center (SBDC) network. Offices are present in every state and the District of Columbia. SBDCs are valuable sources of free information and advice for small business owners. The state director's office can refer you to the SBDC nearest you. If you are starting a business, this office is a great resource.

- Appendix C lists national and state-specific business magazines that may prove helpful in your research regarding new business and industry trends, marketing, and business plans. They may also prove helpful in keeping you on top of national and state legislation that may affect your business.

Lightbulb Information

You may have noticed a lightbulb icon sprinkled throughout this book. This icon signals there are some additional thoughts and questions to the activity statement that immediately precedes it.

 The lightbulb information is provided to prompt you to think about related items or issues that may help you accomplish or complete an activity easier and more fully. Hopefully, this information will help you cover more of the business game basics and avoid costly mistakes.

Sometimes, the lightbulb information provides how-to instructions or most likely, it will be stated in a question format to encourage your thinking process and creativity.

Preaddressed Post Cards

At the very end of *Start Your Business*, you will find two sheets of preaddressed post cards that are ready to mail and simply need postage. These post cards request additional information and materials from several different federal and private agencies.

In particular, you may be interested in a new post card regarding electronic bulletin board systems (BBSs) that provide all kinds of information on-line.

By mailing the BBS post card, you will receive information on PSI Research's upcoming BBS, the SBA On-Line, and other on-line services. At your convenience, review the post cards to see if any of them will be of assistance for your business.

The Bottom Line

By reading and working your way through *Start Your Business*, you are going to learn several different aspects of starting a business. From the smallest of details involving business filings and taxes to the larger areas dealing with research and long-term planning, you will come out ahead because of this book's checklists and tips. You will probably learn about requirements you never knew existed, review areas you were familiar with but may have forgotten, and realize various tasks you can do to help you be a better business owner.

In short, *Start Your Business* will guide you to a better opening day and a more informed beginning. Let the business game begin!

Getting Off on the Right Foot — Start-Up Issues

Introduction

Before you start playing any game — whether it is football, chess, or Monopoly — you usually review the basic rules and objectives so you are comfortable about starting the game in the first place. Playing the business game is no different. Chapter 1 helps you learn the basic rules and considerations you will need to know to be more confident about playing and winning the business game.

Depending on your situation, you may have already decided on some of the basic start-up considerations outlined in this chapter. If you have already dealt with some of these issues, this chapter will be a good review of your initial impressions and decisions regarding what it takes to start your own business. If you have not made some of these basic start-up decisions, then Chapter 1 will be a good starting point.

Some of the fundamental questions you may have already answered by now (or which you should answer after reading this chapter) are:

- What will be the legal form of organization for your business? Will your business be a sole proprietorship, a partnership, a corporation, or a limited liability company (LLC)? Refer to the Glossary for definitions of each form.
- Where will you locate your office or place of business?
- How will your office be set up? What equipment will you buy initially?

These questions, of course, are only a few of the many you will need to answer before starting your business. Other issues, such as how much money you will need to get started, how to write your business plan, and how to develop a marketing strategy, are detailed in later chapters. For now, however, the issues and considerations raised in this chapter will help you get off on the right foot.

First Aid for Start-Up Issues

To aid you in the business game, one of the best sources of overall general and specific requirements for starting a business is the *Starting and Operating a Business in ...* series. This series, which features a book for each of the 50 states, plus the District of Columbia, helps you review critical start-up considerations and focus on government requirements for small business. You can obtain the book for your particular state through any major bookstore chain or by calling the publisher directly.

***Starting and Operating a Business in ...* series**
The Oasis Press/PSI Research
Grants Pass, OR
(503) 479-9464
(800) 228-2275

Another excellent source of helpful start-up information is the computer software program, *The Small Business Expert*. This "smart" program asks you questions about your business and instantly creates a detailed, customized, new business start-up checklist for you, listing the various tax and regulatory requirements that you must comply with. *The Small Business Expert* also provides interactive, consulting sessions to help you decide on whether or not to incorporate your business, and similar choices on other complex issues. This software is also available from The Oasis Press/PSI Research.

General Requirements for All New Start Ups

Regardless of whether your business is a sole proprietorship, a partnership, a corporation, or a limited liability company (LLC), you will be required to make certain filings and registrations with government agencies, pay certain taxes, and complete certain research before opening your doors. The first checklist in this section highlights some general start-up considerations to act on as soon as possible, regardless of your business' legal form. This checklist focuses on nongovernmental considerations, whereas the subsequent checklists deal with general government requirements on the federal, state, and local levels.

Additional requirements that apply specifically to sole proprietorships, partnerships, or corporations are outlined in the next section of this chapter, and additional requirements for any business that will hire employees are covered in Chapter 4.

The main goal of this section is to highlight the initial requirements for any business starting up in any state. Review these checklists carefully so you learn the business game basics.

General Start-Up Considerations Checklist

No matter what type of business you will start or what form of legal organization you choose, you will need to think about some general start-up considerations. The activities listed below will provide an initial plan of action.

☐ Determine your legal form of business organization. Review the advantages and disadvantages of each of the forms listed below.

☐ Sole proprietorship

☐ General or limited partnership

☐ Corporation

☐ Limited liability company (LLC)

☐ Learn what it means to elect S corporation status and see if it is a benefit for your business.

☐ List all the possible names for your business. Avoid descriptive names, initials, family surnames, geographic names, and names identical to or very similar to ones already in use.

☐ Rank the top ten names you have listed above, and research them to see which ones are available for use.

☐ Choose the name of your business.

☐ Create a logo for your business, if desired.

☐ Choose the name of your product or service.

☐ Consider the types of insurance you will need to obtain before opening your doors. Refer to Chapter 2 for more guidance on business insurance.

☐ Determine the steps you will take to lessen your personal liability regarding the business.

Will you incorporate to avoid personal liability?

Will you purchase a personal liability policy?

Will you create clear, written company policies to verify your procedures? See Chapter 4 for more on company policies.

☐ Look for reputable accountants and attorneys to work with you.

Do they have satisfied clients who will give recommendations?

Do they have an expertise in business law?

How are their fees compared to others in the local area?

☐ Do a complete financial overview of your start-up venture. Refer to Chapter 2 for more specifics on how to do this. Consider:

How much money will you need for the first six months of operations?

What are your initial start-up expenses?

Where will you get additional sources of funds when necessary?

☐ Determine if your business will need employees. Refer to Chapter 4 for more on what to do if you will have employees.

☐ Write a business plan. Refer to Chapter 7.

☐ Organize your initial marketing strategies. Refer to Chapter 3.

Federal General Requirements Checklist

This checklist covers all the general requirements you should know about when dealing with the federal government as a new business owner, regardless of your business' legal form. Review the checklist carefully to determine what actions you will need to take on behalf of your business. Agencies you need to contact for more information are often listed in parentheses after the activity.

☐ Do a federal trade name, trademark, or service mark search. (Patent and Trademark Office in Washington, D.C.)

☐ Determine if you need a federal license to operate your business.

 Most new small businesses do not require federal licensing. Some of the businesses that do require federal licensing include investment firms, broadcast stations, common carrier companies, firearm dealers, meat packagers, and drug producers.

☐ Obtain information on how and when to make quarterly federal estimated income tax payments. (IRS)

☐ Learn about your obligations for reporting certain federal tax information on the 1099 form series. (IRS)

☐ Review the environmental regulations set forth in the Comprehensive Environmental Response, Compensation and Liability Act (CERCLA or also known as Superfund) and the Resource Conservation and Recovery Act (RCRA). (U.S. Department of Environmental Quality)

State and Local General Requirements Checklist

In addition to the federal requirements listed above, it is equally important all forms of business take care of the general requirements set forth by the appropriate state and local governments. In general, most states have similar registration requirements and taxes; however, each state is unique and you are encouraged to research both state and local requirements through your various state and local agencies or one-stop business centers.

By checking with your local agencies, you will rest much easier knowing you haven't missed any registration or tax not mentioned in this checklist.

☐ Do a state and local trade name search to determine if the name you have chosen for your business, product, or service is identical or confusingly similar to a name that is already in use. To do this:

    ☐ Contact your secretary of state's office and your local county clerk's office to request this information.

    ☐ Look through local phone directories, business directories, and publications for any similar name.

☐ Obtain a local business license from your city hall or county office.

☐ Obtain a state business license, plus any additional licenses that may be required for your particular profession or occupation, from the appropriate state licensing agency.

☐ If your state has an income tax, know how to report your earnings or losses on the appropriate returns.

☐ Determine how to make state estimated income tax filings, if applicable, in your state.

☐ Register your business with the appropriate state revenue or tax department for any required seller's permit or sales tax license, whichever is applicable.

 Is a separate permit required for each place of business?

Where do you need to display the permit(s)?

Are you required to display it on the opening day of business?

☐ Investigate your obligation as a seller for collecting and remitting any sales and use tax in your state.

☐ Determine how to register your fictitious business name with both the state and local governments.

 How does your state define a fictitious business name?

Are you required to publish a notice of doing business under that name in a local newspaper, and what is the fee for registering the name?

Will you have to file an affidavit of publication with any local agency regarding your fictitious business name?

☐ Check on local zoning ordinances, regulations, and other land use restrictions before selecting a site for your new business.

 What signs, if any, can you erect? Is there a size restriction?

Is your proposed business site zoned for commercial use?

What about off-street parking? Will this be a problem?

Will you be able to get city services, such as water and sewer?

Will you need any permits for remodeling or constructing your business?

☐ Contact your state and local tax departments to inquire about any and all taxes you will need to be aware of as a business. Ask about:

☐ Excise taxes on such items as tobacco, fuels, and hazardous substances, if applicable to your particular type of business;

☐ Inventory and equipment taxes;

☐ Motor vehicle registration fees; and

☐ Property taxes.

☐ Research any state or local environmental laws that may apply to your type of business, such as air quality and hazardous waste disposal requirements.

Specific Requirements for Various Legal Forms of Business

Each legal form of doing business has its own advantages and disadvantages, and which one you choose for your new business is a decision only you can make. The four main forms of doing business are:

- Sole proprietorships
- Partnerships
- Corporations
- Limited liability companies (LLCs)

Refer to the Glossary for definitions of these four legal forms of doing business. Once you know which legal form of business you will use, review the appropriate checklist in this section to find out the requirements that are specific to your legal form. Remember you need to do all of the activities listed in the previous section, General Requirements for All New Start Ups, regardless of your legal form. The checklists in this section cover the four main legal forms of doing business respectively.

Sole Proprietorship Checklist

This checklist is for sole proprietorships only. Because sole proprietors have relatively few requirements for starting a business, this checklist is shorter than the others in this section.

☐ Prepare to include *Schedule C* with your federal individual income tax return, *Form 1040*. You are required to report all your income or loss from the business on this return.

☐ If your state has a personal income tax (or an equivalent tax), then research how to report any income or loss from your business on your state tax returns by contacting your state tax department or your accountant.

7

☐ Research the federal self-employment tax by contacting the IRS.

 The self-employment tax is a Social Security and Medicare tax for those who work for themselves. You are required to pay this tax as a sole proprietor, as well as file *Schedule SE* with your *Form 1040* tax return.

☐ Double-check with your secretary of state's office (or its equivalent) to see if there are any additional state registration requirements or filings that weren't included in the State and Local General Requirements Checklist on page 5.

Partnership Checklist

This checklist is for partnerships only. The checklist includes requirements for both general and limited partnerships. Those requirements pertaining to limited partnerships only are indicated by an (LP only) at the end of the requirement. The requirements without the (LP only) following them apply to both general and limited partnerships.

☐ Though not an official requirement by any governmental agency, consider writing a partnership agreement for your partnership.

    ☐ Have this agreement signed by each partner.

    ☐ Have your attorney and accountant review the agreement.

☐ Investigate federal reporting procedures regarding partnership income by contacting the IRS and requesting information on how to:

    ☐ File federal *Form 1065*, a partnership information return; and

    ☐ Report your share of partnership income or loss on your federal income tax return.

☐ If your state has a personal income tax (or an equivalent tax), then research how to report any income or loss from your partnership on your state tax returns by contacting your state tax department or your accountant.

☐ Research the federal self-employment tax by contacting the IRS. The self-employment tax is a Social Security and Medicare tax for those who work for themselves. You are required to pay it as a partner.

☐ Even if your partnership will not have employees, you are still required to file *Form SS-4, Application for Employer Identification Number* (EIN), with the IRS. This filing will register you with the IRS and provide you with the EIN that you will use for tax filing purposes.

☐ File a certificate of limited partnership with your secretary of state's office and see if you are required to file copies of this certificate with the counties in which you plan to do business. (LP only)

   ☐ Check to see if a fee is charged for this filing. (LP only)

☐ Double-check with the secretary of state's office to see if there are any additional state registration requirements for general or limited partnerships that weren't included in the State and Local General Requirements Checklist on page 5.

Corporation Checklist

This checklist is for corporations only. The requirements specific to corporations are definitely more numerous than for sole proprietorships and partnerships. As mentioned earlier, if you plan to incorporate your new business, consulting an attorney to help you through the process is recommended. Review the checklist below and make sure you and your attorney deal with each activity as it applies to your situation.

☐ File your corporation's articles of incorporation with your secretary of state's office.

☐ Check with the appropriate state agency — usually the secretary of state's office — to see what fees are required for incorporation.

☐ Adopt a set of bylaws.

☐ Designate a registered office or registered agent who can and will be available for the service and process of official correspondence from the courts or state governments to your corporation.

☐ Ensure that your corporate name includes the word, "corporation," "incorporated," "company," "limited," or "association."

☐ Decide if your corporation will issue stock.

What kinds of stock are there and which ones do you want to offer?

How will your corporation pay out dividends?

How will your shareholders' agreement be drawn up?

Which securities laws will you need to comply with?

☐ Elect a board of directors and schedule when it will meet.

   ☐ Ensure someone will be responsible for taking minutes of the meeting and distributing them accordingly.

- [ ] Keep detailed corporate records once your corporation has begun to operate. This will include records such as:
  - [ ] The minutes from all board of director and shareholder meetings;
  - [ ] A record of all actions taken by the board of directors or shareholders without a meeting;
  - [ ] All written communication by the corporation to the shareholders;
  - [ ] A list of the names and addresses of current officers and directors; and
  - [ ] The most recent annual report of the corporation that was submitted to the secretary of state.

- [ ] If you will do business outside your state of incorporation, obtain a certificate of authority from each state where you plan to do business. A certificate of authority can be obtained through the secretary of state's office in each state where you plan to do business.
  - [ ] Pay any appropriate fees for these filings.
  - [ ] Include a certificate of good standing with your filing information. This certificate is available through the secretary of state's office in the state where you incorporate.

- [ ] Contact the IRS to receive instructions on how to report corporate income tax on *Form 1120*.

- [ ] Obtain plenty of federal tax deposit coupons from the IRS so your corporation can make its estimated income tax payments easily.

- [ ] File *Form SS-4, Application for Employer Identification Number*, with the IRS to receive your employer identification number. You must do this filing even if you don't have employees.

- [ ] Contact the state tax department to receive instructions on how to pay its corporate income or franchise tax.

 Will you have to pay estimated payments for any state income tax? What is the minimum amount for any franchise tax in your state?

- [ ] Request that the state tax department send you information on all the corporate tax requirements within the state. This will ensure you don't forget anything regarding the state's tax requirements for corporations.

- [ ] Know the difference between an S corporation, a foreign corporation, and a professional service corporation.

☐ Register with your state's secretary of state, tax authority, and other agencies to receive a business account number.

☐ Make a note that your corporation must file annual reports once it is up and running.

☐ Comply with both state and federal securities laws.

Limited Liability Company Checklist

This checklist is for limited liability companies (LLCs) only. This form of doing business is now available in the District of Columbia and in every state — except for Hawaii, Massachusetts, and Vermont. Because it is such a relatively new form of doing business, requirements for its organization vary from state to state; however, this checklist provides some basic overall LLC requirements.

To find out more regarding this new form of doing business, you can get a copy of *The Essential Limited Liability Company Handbook* from The Oasis Press.

☐ File articles of organization with your secretary of state's office.

☐ Because nearly all states require an LLC to have at least two owners, consider who will be your co-owner.

☐ Check with the appropriate state agency — usually the secretary of state's office — to see what fees and registration are required for an LLC.

☐ If your state has an income tax (or an equivalent tax), then research how to report any income or loss of your LLC on your state and federal tax returns by contacting your local tax or revenue department.

☐ Double-check with the secretary of state's office to see if there are any additional state registration requirements for limited liability companies that weren't included in the State and Local General Requirements Checklist on page 5.

Location! Location! Location!

Deciding where to locate your business can often mean the difference between winning the business game and losing it. You may have the highest-quality product or the most helpful service in your area, but if you don't locate your business appropriately, you can lose a lot of money through missed foot traffic opportunities or an insufficient pool of qualified labor.

The reasons to locate in a certain place vary depending on your type of business. For example, if you are going to open a restaurant or retail business, you are obviously going to want to ideally locate in an area where there is a lot of available parking, a good flow of walk-in and drive-by traffic, and little competition.

If you are a manufacturer or wholesaler, you will be more interested in a site that is close to major transportation services, has a large pool of skilled labor available, and has sufficient access to water, sewer, and other vital services.

Lastly, if you are going to be one of the millions of people who are starting their business out of their homes, then your location considerations are basically concerned with knowing zoning and land use restrictions in your neighborhood. You will need to know what you can and cannot do in terms of shipping and receiving, signage, business activity, and remodeling in your particular residential area.

The three checklists in this section help cover some of the activities you should consider when deciding where to locate your business. The first checklist features general considerations for nearly all types of businesses, while the remaining two checklists deal with considerations for specific types of businesses, namely, retail and nonretail businesses.

General Location Considerations Checklist

This checklist is a potpourri of tips and activities you can consider when deciding where to locate your new business in a particular place. Most of these considerations apply to all types of businesses, with the possible exception of home-based businesses. Regardless of your type of business, reviewing this checklist will be beneficial and valuable when considering opening your own business.

☐ Consider the advantages of leasing your place of business, such as less financial risk and the option of subletting, or avoiding a long-term rental commitment. If you do decide to lease your business' location, consider including the following items in any agreement you sign:

☐ The length of the lease;

☐ The amount of rent, how it is determined, and when it is payable;

☐ The description of the space to be occupied;

☐ The option to renew;

- ☐ Any restrictions on remodeling or other modifications to the interior of the space and who owns any leasehold improvements;

- ☐ Any restrictions on the posting of signs on the outside of the building or in the surrounding yard;

- ☐ Protection from co-occupancy or nearby occupancy by competing businesses;

- ☐ The option to purchase the space;

- ☐ Landlord responsibilities regarding improvements for fire, health, and safety issues;

- ☐ Insurance requirements for the landlord and tenant;

- ☐ Reconstruction timing and requirements in case of fire, earthquake, or other natural disasters;

- ☐ Status of tenant, if the space is sold; and

- ☐ The possibility of subletting by the tenant.

☐ Always have your attorney review any real estate or lease agreements.

☐ Research any environmental restrictions that may apply to your business if it locates in a particular area.

☐ Ensure your type of business can locate in a particular area by reviewing its zoning laws.

☐ Determine the kind of security system you will need to install by investigating the crime rate in your location and talking to law enforcement officials.

☐ Determine the cost of purchasing the real estate as opposed to leasing it.

 How do the costs compare for the short and long term?

Are there any advantages to doing one over the other?

☐ Be sure to investigate only the sites most appropriate for your type of business. For instance, as a manufacturer, don't waste a lot of time looking at prime downtown retail locations; concentrate on industrial parks or other such avenues.

☐ See if any local economic development agency is available to help you find a suitable site.

☐ Contact the local governments — for example, the city hall or county clerk's office — to determine what, if any, taxes or permits will apply to your business within a particular area.

☐ Find a real estate agent to help you look for a possible site for your business.

☐ Find out what energy sources are available at each site and whether they are adequate for your type of machinery, equipment, or production process.

Are the energy costs within your budget?

Can you get alternative energy sources, if you so desire?

What is involved in setting up a business account with the public utilities available in your area?

What is the usual waiting period for receiving utility services?

☐ Evaluate each site as it is now, and then try to forecast how it will be situated within the short- and long-term future.

Is there a possibility of residential development nearby?

What are the population trends for the area? Are they increasing or decreasing?

What is the water source like? Is it dependable?

Can you expand or reduce your space easily?

Do you anticipate commercial growth in that area?

Is there additional space or property you could purchase in the future?

Retail Location Considerations Checklist

If you are going to be operating a retail store or another type of business that is going to rely heavily on foot traffic, then this checklist is for you. Review the considerations outlined below before deciding where to locate your business.

☐ Review the following basic aspects for any potential retail or service business site you are considering:

    ☐ Research the population trends for the local county or city to see if your particular business will have enough support, in terms of a potential market, to survive.

    ☐ Determine the number of competitors already established in the area and whether or not any more plan to locate there.

Is the area too saturated with competitors to be a good site?

Is being too close to competitors beneficial or hurtful to your new business?

☐ Study the reaction of the local community to businesses similar to yours.

Was the response favorable, or did the community tend to stay with the more established business?

Is your type of business considered "undesirable" to the local neighborhood or community? If so, consider another area.

☐ Evaluate how accessible the site is for walk-in or drive-by traffic.

Is there plenty of parking around your location?

Are mass transit stops nearby?

Are all the popular shops on your side of the street? Or will people have to cross the street to come to your door?

Is the location near a tricky intersection where it is difficult to make a turn into your business?

☐ Determine if the site's atmosphere and physical surroundings attract or detract the type of customers you are seeking.

☐ Make sure the zoning restrictions in your location's area are such that other businesses can move in to enhance your location.

☐ Research the foot traffic and the automobile traffic that is going by your potential site.

Are the numbers good enough to warrant consideration?

How is your target market reflected in those numbers?

☐ Compare the cost of each site to determine which is the most cost-effective.[1]

☐ Ensure you will have enough space for your needs.

☐ Find out how close you are to major boulevards, highways, shopping centers, and civic centers to make sure your business location is visible and easily accessible.

☐ Determine how close you are to fire and police departments and what kind of protection is available.

---

1. The information listed under this first activity has been paraphrased from the publication, *Starting a Successful Business on the West Coast* (pages 22–27), which is written by Douglas L. Clark, and published by Self-Counsel Press, 1992.

☐ Make sure the space has or will have nice restrooms and other appropriate employee/customer facilities.

☐ Determine how the location and facilities enhance your business' image.

Nonretail Location Considerations Checklist

If you will have a manufacturing, wholesale, or mail order business, then your location considerations will be different than those listed for retailers and service businesses. Since your business will not rely heavily on foot traffic or walk-in customers, you will want to look more at the physical aspects of any location or site to ensure it specifically meets all your business' needs. When looking at available sites, think about each of the factors listed below to help you in your decision making.

☐ Ensure that the physical aspects of the site are what you need.

Is there room to expand if necessary?

Are there any bogholes, swamps, or other similar problems with the ground surface?

Are there any awkward slopes, rocky spots, or timber to be removed?

☐ See if the location is conveniently situated in a geographic area that is easy to get to and not too far out of the way for both you and any employees you will hire.

☐ Research the availability of skilled labor in the area.

Will there be an adequate supply of the types of skilled workers you will need for your type of business?

☐ Determine if any building you evaluate or build has:

☐ Employee restrooms, break areas, or designated smoking areas;

☐ Enough space for start-up operations, plus room to grow;

☐ Enough electrical outlets and power capability for your company's needs, such as for computers, production equipment, and heating and air conditioning;

☐ Complied with all accessibility requirements under the Americans with Disabilities Act (ADA);

☐ An adequate shipping and receiving area that can accommodate the type of transportation services you will be using;

☐ Plenty of phone jacks and lines to handle all your business calls; and

☐ Sound structural design.

☐ See who your neighbors will be and if they are competitors or compatible businesses.

☐ Find the suppliers you will need for your business and see if the location is convenient for them.

☐ Ensure the availability of raw materials, adequate sanitation, and utilities.

☐ See how convenient the location is for any transportation services you will use for your business.

Is it out of the way for delivery and pickup trucks?

Are you near an airport, railroad station, or water port? Which ones are the most important for you to be near?

☐ Determine what support services you will need to run your business and see if your business location is convenient for all concerned. For instance:

Where is your office supplier located?

Where are necessary repair services located?

Office Set Up

Once you have decided where your business will be located, you should start thinking about getting your business office in order. Again, the factors involved in this are going to vary depending on your type of business.

For instance, if you will be operating a home-based business, your needs can be very simple or elaborate, depending on your clients, product, or service. If you will be delivering baked goods to local stores, then your office needs will be minimal, but if you will have clients coming to your home office to review projects or learn more about your product or service, then a more professional office setting, including interior design and furniture, may be appropriate.

If you will be operating a retail, manufacturing, wholesale, or service company, you will still want to present a professional appearance, but the degree of this appearance will vary depending on your situation and finances.

For the most part, this section prompts you to think about how you will set up your office physically and with what kinds of equipment and office furniture. In addition, some basic office procedures are included to get you thinking about how your office can be managed and organized.

When first starting your business, try to buy only those supplies necessary for start up. You will want to spend wisely at this point and you can always buy more supplies as your needs warrant. Make sure you are prepared financially for your initial start-up office costs, and be sure to include these expenses in your budgeting process. See Chapter 2 for more on money matters.

Office Set Up Checklist

Take the time to review this checklist and begin to formulate an idea of how you would like to have your office organized. Remember this is a general checklist and your type of business may warrant some special equipment, furniture, or supplies not listed. Try to think what these items could be so you can anticipate buying them for your first day of operation.

☐ List all your anticipated office furniture needs for initial start up, for example, desks, chairs, file cabinets, and lamps.

Will you need to include interior decorating items, such as plants, rugs, and window coverings?

Will it be more advantageous for you to rent or own your office furniture?

What about the possibility of buying used furniture or new furniture?

☐ List all your anticipated office equipment needs for initial start up, for example, personal computers, fax machines, telephones, typewriters, printers, and copiers. Be sure to list how many of each you will be needing.

_____

_____

_____

_____

_____

_____

_____

☐ Have your business stationery and company logo designed and printed. Other business paperwork you may need to have printed include:

☐ Business cards   ☐ Purchase orders

☐ Business envelopes   ☐ Receipts

☐ Company checks   ☐ Sales orders

☐ Invoices   ☐ Shipping labels

How much will it cost for the design of a logo?

How much will it cost to print your letterhead, invoices, and business cards?

How will you design your company's in-house invoices and purchase orders?

☐ Estimate your office supply needs — such as paper, pens, tape, phone message pads, paper clips, Post-it Notes, calendars, dictionaries, hanging file folders, and staplers — and shop around for the best prices. Include:

☐ Computer supplies and needs, such as computer paper, disks, disk labels, software programs, accessories, toner, and technical support services.

☐ Create a process and get a box for handling petty cash.

☐ Establish a basic form of bookkeeping for your front desk needs.

☐ Obtain a ledger.

☐ Have a cash receipts journal.

☐ Determine how you will purchase postage.

Will you use a postage meter or purchase stamps?

What is your monthly estimate for postage expenses?

☐ Contact your local post office and get general information on how to:

☐ Determine postage amounts for different parcels and letters;

☐ Organize a bulk mailing; and

☐ Use business reply cards.

☐ Choose a delivery service, such as Federal Express or United Parcel Service, and learn about its schedules, fees, and services.

☐ Establish your regular business office hours.

☐ Determine how you or your receptionist will answer the phone.

What greeting will you use?

How will phone transfers be made? Will you transfer directly to each person, or will you screen calls so the person being called knows the name of the person calling?

What kind of holding messages or music will you employ, if any?

☐ Decide if you will use a telephone answering service or machine to answer business calls that come in after hours. Also consider:

How many lines will you need?

Will you have a fax machine?

Will you have voice mail?

What about a toll-free, 800 number?

☐ Investigate the cost and procedure for getting a telephone number for your business and listing that number in the local phone directory.

☐ Set up business letter models for common correspondence applicable to your type of business.

☐ Set up and organize your filing system for the office.

  ☐ Jot down whatever office supplies you will need for this system.

_____

_____

_____

_____

☐ Research where to find the best buys on office furniture and supplies.

Strategies and Tips

Starting your own business is a big decision and one that should not be taken lightly. The chances for success are there, but you will have to work at it. Some of the business basics discussed in this and the following chapters will hopefully lessen your initial concern of covering all the bases before you open your doors. Read the additional strategies and tips below for encouragement and reference. Be sure to complete the Plan of

Action for Start-Up Issues worksheet on page 27 to help organize your start-up thoughts, concerns, and activities.

- Some of the best reasons to start your own business include being your own boss; receiving all the profits from the business; having a sense of independence and personal satisfaction; and being able to work directly with people.

- One of the most important things to consider when starting your new business is to ensure that you, or someone who will be working with you, really knows the business or trade you are starting. This will help establish credibility and smoother sailing in the long run.

- Starting a business requires that you work harder and longer than you did when you were an employee. Be prepared to work more than a nine-to-five schedule and possibly for less money initially.

- Attend as many business seminars, classes, and workshops as you can before starting your business. Find out some of the realities of building a business from scratch or taking over an existing business. Be as informed as possible on what to expect as a new business owner.

- If your business will only have one product or service, consider using the same name for both your business and its product or service. You get double reinforcement every time the name gets printed or is seen by a customer.

- Always have your office area clean and professional looking, regardless of your type of business. Clients, customers, vendors, and suppliers form initial impressions of businesses by how their front or main offices appear.

Helpful Resources

Association of Small Business Development Centers
Omaha, NE
(402) 595-2387
FAX (402) 595-2388

Small Business Development Centers (SBDCs) are terrific resources for any small business getting started. SBDCs are located in various communities throughout every state. Usually associated with community colleges or universities, these centers provide start-up information and conduct business-oriented seminars.

To find the SBDC nearest you, contact the SBDC Association in Omaha, or find the number of your SBDC state director's office from the list provided in Appendix B.

Complete Book of Business Forms
The Oasis Press/PSI Research
Grants Pass, OR 97526
(503) 479-9464
(800) 228-2275

This handy book is a great source of business forms for the beginning business owner. It features ready-to-use forms that cover areas including employee recordkeeping, accounting, and general business office administration. $19.95.

Corporate Agents, Inc.
Wilmington, DE
(800) 877-4224

This company can help you form your corporation in any state for as little as $99, plus state fees. For an additional cost, you can purchase the appropriate corporate seal, minute book, stock certificates, and sample forms and bylaws. Call the above number for more information.

The Essential Corporation Handbook
The Oasis Press/PSI Research
Grants Pass, OR
(503) 479-9464
(800) 228-2275

This book takes the mysteries out of corporate formalities and shows owners what they *must* do and what they *may* do with their corporations. Includes checklists and sample documents and forms. If you are thinking about incorporating your business, this is a must-have book. $19.95.

The Essential Limited Liability Company Handbook
The Oasis Press/PSI Research
Grants Pass, OR
(503) 479-9464
(800) 228-2275

If you are interested in learning more about LLCs, this book will help you do so with its straightforward, easy-to-read discussions on how LLCs compare to other legal entities and how to form an LLC in your state. Features sample LLC documents and a helpful question-and-answer section. $19.95.

Home Business Made Easy
The Oasis Press/PSI Research
Grants Pass, OR
(503) 479-9464
(800) 228-2275

This helpful book provides more than 150 start-up business ideas, plus it discusses basic considerations regarding home-based businesses. It also has handy appendices with listings of helpful resources specifically designed to help the home-based business get off on the right foot. Call the above number for more information. $19.95.

The Legal Guide for Starting and Operating a Small Business
Nolo Press
Berkeley, CA
(510) 549-1976
(800) 992-6656

This guide is a comprehensive coverage of leases, with emphasis on avoiding legal problems. Its discussions cover short- and long-term leases, shopping center leases, additions and modifications, as well as advice on resolving disputes with landlords and getting legal advice. For more information, call the above number. $22.95.

Naming Your Business and Its Products and Services
The P. Gaines Publishing Company
Oak Park, IL
(800) 578-3853

A fun-to-read book on how to name your business. Good tips and advice for selecting a business name and a good source for learning how to research trade names, trademarks, and service marks effectively. $19.95.

National Association for the Self-Employed (NASE)
P.O. Box 612067
DFW Airport, TX 75261-2067
(800) 232-NASE
FAX (800) 551-4446

Founded in 1981, NASE is an action-oriented, nonprofit association committed to helping the self-employed meet the challenges of making their businesses successful. More than 300,000 members give NASE a powerful voice in Washington D.C.

National Business Association (NBA)
P.O. Box 870728
Dallas, TX 75287
(800) 456-0440
FAX (214) 960-9149

A nonprofit organization specifically designed and actively managed to assist the small businessperson in achieving her professional and personal goals. The NBA offers an array of benefits and services that provide monetary discounts and other quality resources.

National Federation of Independent Business (NFIB)
Attn: Membership Services
53 Century Boulevard
Nashville, TN 37214
(800) NFIB NOW

The NFIB is the nation's largest small business organization, with more than half a million business owner members. The NFIB has been America's small business advocate since 1943 and is dedicated to preserving free enterprise. To find out more regarding this helpful organization, contact Membership Services.

Records Management
American Management Association (AMA)
New York, NY
(518) 891-5510
(800) 225-3215

This book provides guidance on how to perfect the art of recordkeeping, from starting up a program to maintaining a records center, designing filing systems, and handling forms and reports. $29.95.

SBA Answer Desk
U.S. Small Business Administration
Washington, DC
(800) 827-5722

The SBA Answer Desk is a series of prerecorded messages that helps answer many questions new start ups may have about financing or starting a business. You can also request a listing of SBA publications from the SBA Answer Desk.

SBA On-Line
Washington, DC
(800) 697-4636
(900) 463-4636
FAX (202) 205-7064

The SBA has established an electronic computer network to provide information on its programs and services via computer modem. The toll-free number offers access to information on SBA services, loans, business programs, and information from other government agencies 23 hours a day.

Through the low-cost 900 line, users can access e-mail and gateway functions to the Environmental Protection Agency, the Department of Commerce, and the Census Bureau bulletin board services (BBSs). The first minute of connect time is free; $0.30 (30 cents) for the second minute; $0.10 (10 cents) for each additional minute. Telecommunications settings are eight data bits, one stop bit, no parity.

For more information on SBA On-Line, you can refer to the U.S. government section of your local phone directory; for more on other on-line business information services, mail the preaddressed BBS post card provided at the end of this book.

The Small Business Expert
The Oasis Press/PSI Research
Grants Pass, OR
(503) 479-9464
(800) 228-2275

This is a unique, easy-to-use, interactive software program for DOS that gives you concise, up-to-date advice on several hundred subjects, such as business start ups and all types of federal and state taxes and business regulations. It includes customized new business start-up checklists and interactive consulting sessions to help you decide on issues such as setting up a partnership or corporation, purchasing a business, buying a franchise, hiring staff, and maximizing cash flow. $34.95.

Small Business Advancement National Center
Conway, AR
(501) 450-5300

The Small Business Advancement National Center collects and disseminates demographic and statistical information on Small Business Institutes (SBIs). SBIs are located on college campuses throughout the United States and offer you free business assistance while furthering the education of college students; free, confidential consulting; in-depth analysis of your business; and recommendations to various business problems. Contact a university near you to see if it has an SBI, or contact the above number.

Small Business Service Bureau, Inc. (SBSB)
P.O. Box 15014
Worcester, MA 01615-0014
(508) 756-3513
(800) 222-5678

The SBSB is a national small business organization with more than 50,000 members. Founded in 1968, SBSB provides small business owners and self-employed individuals with money-saving group benefits and services, low-cost group insurance programs, management assistance, and legislative advocacy in all the states and Washington, D.C.

Small-Time Operator
Bell Springs Publishing
Laytonville, CA
(707) 984-6746

Overall general start-up book written in everyday language that tackles the technical aspects of starting a business. It is also a workbook that includes bookkeeping instructions and a sample set of ledgers — all especially designed for the small business owner. $14.95.

Starting a Successful Business on the West Coast
Self-Counsel Press
Bellingham, WA
(206) 676-4530
(800) 663-3007

A helpful book with practical advice for those interested in starting a business on the West Coast. Covers topics from finding the best location for a business to setting up proper records. A general discussion of a variety of business topics. $14.95.

Starting and Operating a Business in . . . series
The Oasis Press/PSI Research
Grants Pass, OR
(503) 479-9464
(800) 228-2275

This helpful series of books covers all 50 states, plus the District of Columbia. Updated frequently, each book contains the latest state-specific and federal business information available. Learn about your state's taxes, laws, and the agencies created to help you start and operate your business more successfully! $24.95 for paperback or $29.95 for 3-ring binder.

Starting Up Your Own Business
Liberty Hall Press/Tab Books, Inc.
Blue Ridge Summit, PA
(800) 822-8158

A step-by-step guide that takes you through the critical first steps of starting a business. Written by professionals from the U.S. Small Business Administration, it is a helpful resource for the beginner. $19.95.

Working Solo Sourcebook
Portico Press
New Paltz, NY
(914) 255-7165
FAX (914) 255-2116

This handy, easy-to-use reference book is your gateway to more than 1,200 essential business resources — each ready to guide you on the path to business success. With more than 40 subject headings, you have a large selection of business resources that are nicely organized and easy to locate. A very valuable reference for any new entrepreneur's desk. $14.95.

Plan of Action for Start-Up Issues

Your company will be a:
☐ Sole proprietorship ☐ Partnership ☐ Corporation ☐ LLC

Use this planning tool to organize and prioritize the activities in this chapter that you need to do to start your business. Don't feel you have to list all the activities you have checked off. You can simply start with the top ten most important ones and go from there, or do whatever is easiest for you. Be sure to make plenty of copies of this cut-out worksheet for your planning and organizing activities for this chapter.

Action to be Taken	Begin Date	Who	Deadline

Plan of Action (continued)

Action to be Taken	Begin Date	Who	Deadline

Chapter 2

Money Matters

Introduction

Although the reason many people start a business is to gain economic independence, most new business owners put little effort into financial planning. They have the mistaken belief that it will not be difficult to raise additional money if their business is doing well and making a profit, or if their idea is a sound one.

Whatever reason you have for getting into business, you will not stay in business long unless you make a profit or have an independent source of financing. Therefore, although you may want to devote your energies to developing your products or to servicing your customers, you probably will not be able to do so unless you devote a reasonable effort to understanding your financial position.

Understanding your financial position is what this chapter is about. The chapter is divided into two main sections. The first section covers the issues and activities involved in funding your business, and the second section covers everyday money matters you should anticipate and budget for. The goal of this chapter is to help you avoid the business game pitfall of not preplanning.

Keep in mind almost any new business will likely require more available money than was originally thought necessary. Most businesses soak up money in ways that were never dreamed of, and if you know and expect this from the beginning, you will be better off in the long run.

First Aid for Money Matters

 If you are looking for some additional help in the financing department, you may want to check out *Financing Your Small Business*, written by Art DeThomas. This step-by-step workbook is a good overview of the various methods you can employ to get money through a loan or many other sources of financing. The book features sample financial statements and rule-of-thumb formulas. It is written in easy-to-read language and would be a good starting point.

You can order this book by contacting the publisher directly or by going through your local bookstore.

Financing Your Small Business
The Oasis Press/PSI Research
Grants Pass, OR
(503) 479-9464
(800) 228-2275

You will also want to obtain the services of a good accountant or certified public accountant to aid you in the financial planning process. These professionals' input will prove invaluable when trying to budget and plan for your business' financial future. They are also more experienced in preparing financial reports accurately and in using generally accepted accounting principles (GAAP).

Check out the Helpful Resources located at the end of this chapter for more tips on where to go for additional assistance.

Financing Your Business

You can finance your business in one of two ways — through equity or debt financing. Equity financing occurs when the owner sells interest in the business to outside investors who are interested in the business' potential growth. This type of financing is usually difficult to obtain for new start ups because they have trouble proving their potential for exceptional growth and return on investment.

Debt financing is the most common way to finance a business. This financing occurs when the owner enters into a contractual agreement with a lender to repay the borrowed money, usually at a preset time, with interest. If payment is not received, the lender can take legal action against the owner to collect the amount that is owed.

Possibly the worst thing you can do when you start your business is to find out that you don't have enough money to run the business and to make a living from it. To keep this from happening, determine your financial needs before you start the business, and know what your needs will be after the business is started.

Start-Up Financial Needs Checklist

The first order of business is to think through all the expenses you will need to pay for in order to get started. Keep in mind that as a new business owner, you will often be required to make a full year's payment in advance or pay a deposit to obtain a lease or open an account with various suppliers, vendors, and utilities.

Do your figuring on a separate piece of paper, and use the items featured in this checklist as a starting point for estimating your start-up expenses and needs. Write down every start-up expense you can think of and be as thorough as possible. Be sure to research which items will require advance payment and estimate the amount you will need for each expense you list.

Consider the following items for your list:

☐ List all your office set up needs by completing the Office Set-Up Checklist on page 18.

☐ List all the production equipment and supplies you will need to produce your product.

☐ Include all the expenses involved in getting a sign for your business.

☐ List all the deposits you may have to pay to receive a necessary service or item. Think about:

    ☐ Electricity or natural gas services

    ☐ Office equipment

    ☐ Office furniture

    ☐ Rent or security deposits for your office space or building

    ☐ Telephone service hook up

    ☐ Water and sewer services

☐ Think about and budget for your insurance needs. See page 41 for more information on business insurance.

☐ Determine what business accounts you will need and if there are any initial account set-up fees.

What suppliers will you need and how do you set up accounts with them?

What will it cost to start up a checking account for your business? What about getting a credit card for your business?

☐ If your business will have employees, determine what expenses will be involved for the first month of operation. Refer to Chapter 4 for more tips on initial employee expenses. Consider:

☐ Payroll taxes

☐ Recruitment costs

☐ Training costs

☐ Wages and benefits

☐ Workers' compensation insurance

☐ Investigate what start-up fees — such as licensing and registration fees — will be required with the state and local governments. Refer to Chapter 1 for start-up requirements.

☐ List all the inventory items (and their costs) you will need to ensure a good start in production, order fulfillment, or service performance.

☐ List all your initial advertising and marketing costs. Refer to Chapter 3 for more on how to plan for your initial marketing strategies.

What form of advertising do you want to use initially? A direct mail piece, newspaper ad, or flyer?

How much will it cost to produce the advertisement?

How much will it cost to distribute or run the advertisement?

What resources will be involved for tracking the ad's effectiveness?

☐ Investigate fees for such things as:

☐ Your business license(s);

☐ Incorporating your business, if applicable;

☐ Franchise packages, if applicable;

☐ Lawyer and accountant services;

☐ Membership fees for trade and industry organizations and associations;

☐ Resource materials, such as how-to business books and business seminars; and

☐ Other activities and needs particular to your own business.

Cash Needs Checklist

After determining the business' expenses, think about your income estimates for the first years following the opening of your business. You may find you don't need to go to a bank for a loan, but to know this, you will need to do a cash-flow projection for the business.

Some lenders and consultants will refer to any financial sheet projections as "pro formas." This is a term used to designate future financial estimates for a business rather than basing figures on numbers from past experience. You can do pro formas for your future balance sheets, income statements, and cash-flow projections. These are valuable tools for determining your income estimates. Consider completing this activity with your financial adviser.

When trying to determine how much money it will take to start your business, estimating your cash needs is an obvious step. You need to be as comprehensive and as thorough as possible when determining how much it will take to start your business. See the Helpful Resources section at the end of this chapter for more on a software program called *Start A Business* that can help you with your projections.

☐ Estimate your personal cash needs for the coming three years.

☐ Look at your household budgets for the past couple of years, then determine what changes you expect in that budget for the coming years, after the business is up and running.

 What additional expenses do you see the business costing you personally?

What is the estimated total of your personal expenses after the business opens?

☐ Use the information from the above activity to help you estimate the amount of salary or draw you will need from the business to cover your personal expenses and to make a living.

☐ Estimate your sales from the business for the next three years.

☐ Prepare a pro forma cash-flow projection, income statement, and balance sheet for the next three years for the business. (See definitions in the Glossary.) Try to answer the following questions when preparing these reports:

When do your business plan projections indicate you will be able to draw a salary from the business? How much will it be?

How are you estimating your sales? Are you being optimistic or pessimistic?

What changes will occur during the coming year that may affect your sales both negatively or positively?

☐ List the sources of cash you have available to you for the coming three years and specify how much money you can count on from them.

_____

_____

_____

_____

_____

_____

Will these sources influence your cash-flow projection?

Are these sources reliable?

Can these sources of income lead you to additional sources?

Sources of Financing Checklist

If you find out you will need to get some additional funding for your business, you have several options. As a small business owner, you may either want short- or long-term financing. The good news is there are several sources of funding for both types.

Of course, the most obvious source of funding for your new start up is yourself and the personal capital and equity you have available. The next available source is often your family, friends, or other business partners. If these sources are not enough or you want to ensure additional funding, review this checklist for ideas on where to go for more money. For a listing of funding sources, refer to *The Money Connection* by Lawrence Flanagan.

☐ If you are interested in short-term funding, the following sources are available to you:

    ☐ Commercial banks

    ☐ Commercial finance companies

☐ Factoring companies (See Glossary for definitions.)

☐ Small Business Investment Companies (SBICs)

☐ State and local economic development programs

☐ U.S. Small Business Administration (SBA)

☐ If you are interested in long-term financing, check out the following possibilities:

   ☐ Commercial banks

   ☐ Commercial finance companies

   ☐ Equipment manufacturers

   ☐ Independent leasing companies

   ☐ Life insurance companies

   ☐ Savings and loan institutions

   ☐ U.S. Small Business Administration

   ☐ Venture capitalists

☐ Investigate the possibility of offering the sale of common stock or securities for your business.

   ☐ Contact the Securities and Exchange Commission (SEC) for more information on securities laws.

Going to a Lender (or Investor) Checklist

Which type of financing you choose to pursue will depend in part on your type of business, your working capital needs, your business' potential for growth, and your attitude about having partners involved in your business. When you decide to go to a lender, having a completed financing proposal in hand will prove very effective in helping you secure a loan.

A financing proposal is the primary document used for securing loans. If you will be going to an investor, however, you may need a private placement circular, a public offering circular, or a limited partnership offering, depending on your situation.

Since most new start ups will be attempting to secure a loan, the brief checklist below focuses on how to prepare a financing proposal. To get more information and to study several examples of financing proposals, refer to *Raising Capital: How to Write a Financing Proposal* by Lawrence Flanagan.

☐ Any financing proposal needs to tell the who, what, why, where, and when about your business.

    ☐ Your content should be brief, but informative.

☐ Write your financing proposal in the third person — that is, don't use "I," "we," or "us" points of view. Be formal and professional in your tone and perspective.

☐ When seeking equity financing, always include the risk factors in your document so investors are warned of potential losses, and make sure the document also includes any information required by the SEC, your state's securities department, and your underwriter.

☐ When going to a lender for a loan or an investor for equity financing, compile all the financial statements regarding your business:

    ☐ Always bring supporting documents to back up any cash or expense projections, such as for sales, profit and loss, and cash flow.

    ☐ Have your projected (pro forma) financial statements prepared for at least three years into the future.

    ☐ Consider whether to have your financial statements audited. Audited statements are required for public stock offerings and limited partnership offerings and are also occasionally requested by banks.

    ☐ If you have a new start up, be prepared to provide copies of your personal income tax returns for at least the previous three years.

☐ If you plan to apply for a loan, you need to anticipate the following:

    ☐ The amount to be repaid each month; and

    ☐ The possible increase in payments.

☐ Your financing proposal for any lender should include the following components:

    ☐ A cover page;

    ☐ A table of contents;

    ☐ A concise summary of the proposal;

    ☐ A brief history of the company, which can include its organization type, the loan that is needed, and how the proceeds will be used;

    ☐ A description of the company, which can include information on current ownership, its product or service, the competition, your background, employees, patents, and the property and equipment you own.

☐ Financial statements, including current balance sheets, profit and loss statements, income statements, and any pro forma statements; and

☐ Related exhibits, which can include letters of support, testimonials, company literature, or photographs.

☐ Review sample financing proposals (or offerings and circulars) to get a feel for how to organize and write your proposal.

☐ Regardless of whether you are going for a loan or for equity financing, you should also create a business plan and take it with you to your prospective lender or investor. See Chapter 7 for more information on what a business plan entails.

Finding the Right Banker Checklist

Banks, like most businesses, are constantly looking for customers. You, as a new business owner, are a potential customer and have the right to see what banks will offer you for your banking business. Most banks offer similar services, but their prices for providing the services may vary considerably. In some cases, you will not be able to get comparable services from one bank to the other.

So, shop for a bank like you shop for any other item. Find out which bank will offer you the most in a package to get your business, but be prepared to give the banker the information that is expected. Such information could include expected deposits per month, expected credit card activity per month, and expected loan requirements.

☐ Research the local phone directory to make a list of the banks nearest you.

☐ Determine which banks you are interested in learning more about.

☐ Set up interviews with each bank's small business department or loan officer.

☐ Interview financial institutions to see which ones are willing to give you the most for your business. Some questions to ask during this interview could include:

How can you reduce checking costs?

Can you transfer money from interest-bearing accounts to checking accounts by phone?

Will you get free cashier's checks or money orders?

Can you get reduced fees for cashing international checks or other instruments, such as a letter of credit?

☐ Compare checking account services and fees.

    ☐ Ask about the bank's monthly, per-check, and account analysis charges for its checking services.

☐ Ask the bank about its services and fees for the following:

    ☐ Equipment loans

    ☐ International money transfers

    ☐ Inventory loans

    ☐ Overdrafts

    ☐ Returned checks

☐ Ask about your options for investing surplus cash without tying it up.

☐ Check out potential investment opportunities at the bank.

 If your company generates enough extra cash, you may want to invest in real estate or mutual funds.

☐ Inquire about floor plan financing, accounts receivable financing, and lines of credit as available options for your business. See the Glossary for definitions of each.

☐ If you plan to build a plant or retail store, you will need a construction loan before the permanent financing. See if the bank provides both forms of financing.

☐ Check how the bank will treat a real estate loan. You may want to ask questions such as:

 How much will the bank charge for points, interest, and fees?

Can you prepay without a penalty?

Is it a fixed payment loan?

Is it a fixed-rate or variable-rate loan?

☐ Ask about credit card arrangements with the bank for the credit card companies listed below.

    ☐ VISA

    ☐ Diners Club

    ☐ Discover

    ☐ MasterCard

☐ American Express

☐ Other: _____

☐ Be sure to ask about charge-back procedures on all the credit cards you are considering signing up for. Different card companies have different policies regarding your ability to protest a charge and how they will deal with crediting you for overcharges and errors in your billing.

Everyday Business Money Matters

Many consultants say the primary cause of business failure is lack of funding. If that is true, then a close second is because an owner doesn't pay enough attention to the ongoing financial condition of the company and operates on a crisis-management basis. He waits until bills are due before realizing that funds are not available to pay them. That is usually not the best time to seek financial help. Additionally, knowing where your money is going so that you can plug unnecessary leaks of cash will add to your profit and prevent undue crises.

This section will remind you of some of the basic everyday money matters that will affect your cash flow. Hopefully, these areas are ones you have already thought about in your estimating of cash needs and listing of start-up expenses. If not, let the checklists in this section serve as helpers for getting you to think about or budget for various business items that can slip through the cracks when first starting a business.

Credit Policy and Collection Techniques Checklist

Deciding whether to extend credit to customers and suppliers can be a tough decision for many new start ups. Extending the credit is easy, but there are definite risks involved, and the collection of the money can be difficult. If you do decide to extend credit, the first step is to develop your company's credit policy. In addition, you should also think about ways you will try to collect any overdue accounts. Remember, there is no right or wrong credit policy or collection technique; every small business is unique and faces different challenges.

The checklist below features general credit and collection tips and activities that can help you get organized in these areas. If you would like more information on credit and collection, refer to The Oasis Press book, *Collection Techniques for a Small Business.*

☐ Determine whether your business will be financially able to offer credit or if it will need to operate on a cash-only basis.

☐ If you extend credit, develop a credit policy that includes the following information:

    ☐ Consider the amount of deposit you will accept and how you will want the remainder of money owed to be paid, for example, cash only or by billing the customer.

    ☐ Decide if you will accept checks, and if so, determine your process and what identifications or verifications you will require.

    ☐ Decide if you will accept credit cards, and if so, choose which ones you will accept, and how you will conduct credit checks.

    ☐ Detail your credit terms, such as discounts for early payment or penalties for late payments.

    ☐ Indicate what it will take for a customer or supplier to qualify for credit.

    ☐ Create a new client (supplier) questionnaire to help you gather important information on potential creditors.

☐ Once you develop a credit policy, explain it thoroughly to all your employees; this will ensure consistency.

☐ Anticipate what it will cost to run credit checks and include the cost in any preplanning budget.

☐ To help collect any debt effectively, consider the following key principles regarding collection techniques:

    ☐ Follow up within five days after a payment is due. Be sure to check that day's mail before calling.

    ☐ Set up your own follow-up system for collecting debts, and always be consistent in your follow up.

    ☐ Develop a strong recordkeeping system to keep track of your phone conversations and written correspondence regarding debt collection.

    ☐ Treat a debtor in a friendly, respectful manner on the first couple of contacts.

    ☐ Be careful to follow the legal and ethical guidelines for debt collecting. For example, do not harass a debtor or make an effort to ruin his reputation.

    ☐ Always ask for payment in full, but be ready and willing to suggest partial payment alternatives and be flexible with any alternatives offered by the debtor.

☐ Motivate and work with the debtor to help her pay the debt by appealing to basic human needs, such as pride, honor, and integrity.

☐ Try to maintain your customer's or supplier's goodwill while you work on getting your money.

Recordkeeping Checklist

Who will do your day-to-day bookkeeping? Many accountants tell stories of clients coming into their office on January 2 with a shoebox of receipts and a checkbook and telling the accountant or bookkeeper to "Do my taxes." What these clients may or may not know is that it will cost them a lot more to have the accountant sort things out than if they did it themselves, or had their bookkeeper do it on a monthly basis, and then take the organized information to the accountant.

☐ Choose the person responsible for doing your financial records.

 Will this be the same person who will do your payroll?

Will this person be responsible for preparing all payroll reports, such as for FUTA, income tax withholdings, FICA, and workers' compensation?

☐ Consider if a fiscal year end or calendar year end is more advantageous for your business.

☐ Determine the kind of accounting system you will use in your business.

 If you have a personal computer, what type of software package best fits your needs? Be sure to compare and shop around.

If you do not have a personal computer, what type of hand accounting system will you use?

☐ Choose the person responsible for completing reports for reasons such as:

☐ Reports to banks or financial institutions;

☐ Taxes for local, state, federal governments; and

☐ Corporate reports to state and federal governments.

Business Insurance Checklist

Buying insurance for your business is an important financial decision and one you need to consider in any preplanning budget and expense projections. The keys for buying business insurance include preparing to shop; deciding which agents/brokers will provide you with price quotes; and picking the best coverage, service, and price combination for your business needs.

The checklist below, which is based on The Oasis Press book, *The Buyer's Guide to Business Insurance*, by Don Bury and Larry Heischman, will give you an outline of basic prepurchase items you can do to make your business insurance purchase an economical and comprehensive one.

☐ Gather information about your business and its insurance needs and use it to streamline the quote process and get the most coverage for your dollar. Information to gather includes:

   ☐ A general company history, if any; and a thorough description of your current or projected operations; and annual projected payroll, sales or receipts;

   ☐ Copies of existing insurance policies, leases, and marketing and business plans;

   ☐ Copies of loss runs from insurance companies if you are purchasing an existing business;

   ☐ The dates you want all of your policies to begin and expire;

   ☐ Information about and descriptions of such items as the buildings you occupy (even if you rent), machinery and equipment, and employee-owned property on your premises (like a mechanic's tools);

   ☐ A list of all vehicles used in the business; include the year, make, model, cost new, use of each unit, and the distance they are driven on a normal day; and

   ☐ Copies of your driving records, and those of any family members who drive your business vehicles, and those of all your employees.

☐ Get to know what types of insurance sellers there are in the insurance industry's marketplace, as well as their respective duties and specialties.

   ☐ Choose several well-educated, experienced agents or brokers, or both, with whom to shop for your purchase. Ask for referrals from your friendly competitors; your national, state, or local associations; or your chamber of commerce.

   ☐ Try to build a favorable rapport with insurance sellers as you work to reduce your price and increase service.

   ☐ Find out how insurance companies are rated and how financially stable they are.

   ☐ Learn the difference between an admitted and a nonadmitted insurance company.

   ☐ Select the insurance companies you want to insure your business.

- ☐ Know your business insurance coverage options by familiarizing yourself with the following:

  - ☐ Determine if you should insure all of your vehicles or not.

     What does the state and your bank require?

    Do you need physical damage on all of them?

  - ☐ Investigate commercial general liability insurance, which protects you from lawsuits from incidents, such as injuries to the general public on your business' premises or damage caused to other people's property by your products, operations, or pollution.

  - ☐ Know where you can buy workers' compensation insurance. Your options may include the state or private companies, or both. See Chapter 4 for more on workers' compensation insurance.

  - ☐ Determine the practicality of coverage for earthquakes, flood, building ordinances and laws, glass, and pollution.

  - ☐ Know the difference between replacement cost versus actual cash value.

  - ☐ Ask about coverage for any property in transit or any special equipment that might break down, and, as a result, jeopardize the entire operation.

  - ☐ Determine if you want special coverage for your computer system.

  - ☐ Determine costs for coverage for theft losses from employees.

  - ☐ Familiarize yourself on coverage for loss of business income caused by a loss to your property.

  - ☐ Compare deductibles to the amount of savings in premium.

  - ☐ Consider whether or not you will need a bond to secure a license or contract.

- ☐ Once you investigate all the different types of available insurance coverage, work with your agents and brokers to compile your coverage checklist.

- ☐ When negotiating price, remember.

  - ☐ Agents and brokers don't get paid unless you buy from them, thus putting you in an excellent position to negotiate.

  - ☐ An informed buyer with her information well compiled is empowered to shop easily and deserves and demands the best possible price and service.

☐ The agent or broker gets his commission out of your purchase price.

☐ Check if the insurance company offers an installment payment plan. This may be less expensive and more convenient than paying the premium up front, or using outside premium financing.

Financial Management Checklist

If you plan to start a one- or two-person operation, the idea of financial management may seem unnecessary for your business preplanning. Simply doing your own books or hiring an accountant may be as far as you want to plan at first; however, once your business begins to grow, financial management will and should become an important part of your responsibilities. Eventually, you will need to move beyond the basics of financial accounting and get involved personally with managing your money and developing strong, working relationships with your financial advisers and managers.

The checklist below is a brief overview of the factors that will help you take control of your company's financial management. The checklist is based on information featured in *Bottom Line Basics*, by Robert Low, which is an excellent resource on financial management. Anticipate doing some of the following activities now and in the future to help ensure strong financial management leadership.

☐ Develop at least a one-year projection for your company, broken down by months, that includes:

    ☐ A balance sheet;

    ☐ A cash-flow statement;

    ☐ An income statement; and

    ☐ A 13-week cash-flow forecast, broken down by weeks, if needed.

☐ Use this projection to determine:

    ☐ How much financing you require;

    ☐ Your break-even level of sales; and

    ☐ The impact on profits of different levels of sales and expenses.

☐ Monitor actual performance against the plan.

    ☐ Revise the plan as needed.

☐ Automate you accounting system.

    ☐ Determine the type of software needed.

☐ Determine how often formal financial statements are needed.

☐ Establish a deadline to have monthly financial statements finished by the seventh working day of the following month and take time to analyze the results.

☐ Develop daily or weekly flash reports that capture key business indicators.

    ☐ These indicators may include nonfinancial measures, such as number of sales leads, percent of capacity used, or units produced.

☐ Focus on cash flow.

    ☐ Establish credit policies and follow up promptly on past due accounts.

    ☐ Maximize inventory turnover and monitor the levels and salability of stock on hand.

☐ Establish internal controls that ensure separation of duties for transactions, especially cash disbursements.

    ☐ Create logs for sales orders, purchase orders, invoices, and shipments.

    ☐ Have all cash accounts reconciled monthly.

☐ Calculate your costs and determine target profit margins.

    Are you charging enough for your products or services?

    How much do you charge to cover overhead expenses, such as space, support staff, and equipment?

    At what markup will you be able to pay all fixed and variable costs?

☐ Clarify the roles of your key accounting and finance people, such as your bookkeeper, accountant, controller, and certified public accountant.

☐ Retain the services of a good financial adviser to help you in your financial management preplanning process.

Tax-Saving Tips Checklist

One way you can help your new start up succeed in money matters is to begin developing tax-saving strategies before you even open your doors. In today's tax environment, you need to be tax savvy and be prepared to deal with the new, methodical tax rules of the business game. This checklist is based on very handy and helpful tax information contained in the business guide, *Top Tax Saving Ideas for Today's Small Business*, written by Thomas

Stemmy. Use this checklist as a starting point for educating and familiarizing yourself with ways to plan for and save on your taxes.

☐ Understand the tax advantages and disadvantages of the type of business entity you choose for your business, for example, sole proprietorship or corporation. Consider:

 Does the new 36 percent income tax rate for individuals making $115,000 a year (or $200,000 for married couples) make the idea of incorporating more attractive since corporate tax rates can be as low as 15 percent?

How do fringe benefits, such as health and accident plans, make the corporation an attractive way to operate your business?

☐ Educate yourself on what the IRS considers as a legitimate business write-off.

  ☐ Discover how fringe benefits to employees can prove to be valuable tax advantages.

☐ Know when and how much to pay on your estimated income taxes so you can avoid possible penalties and interest.

☐ Under the current law, most individuals have learned that they can no longer get a full tax deduction benefit for business and professional expenses. Learn how you can legally regain this tax advantage. See your accountant on this, or refer to Chapter 6 of *Top Tax Saving Ideas for Today's Small Business*.

☐ Don't take business deductions for granted; you, alone, are responsible for providing proof that you are entitled to the write-off. To help do this:

  ☐ Claim your deductions in the right year.

  ☐ Pay by check whenever possible and keep receipts of cash transactions.

  ☐ Record all business mileage and telephone usage.

☐ If you will be operating your business from your home, research the details regarding the home office expense deduction. This is a very misinterpreted part of the tax law, so make sure you get up-to-date advice on how it applies to your particular situation.

☐ Investigate how income-splitting could be of benefit to your tax strategy.

☐ Familiarize yourself with the new tax rules — for example, the Budget Reconciliation Act of 1993 — by reading updated tax publications or discussing them with your accountant or certified public accountant.

☐ Get professional advice on how to do estate planning in connection with one of your most important assets — your business operations. By doing this now, you can ensure a secure future for you and your family and receive tax savings at the same time.

☐ Determine what retirement planning and tax deferrals you can implement into your tax-saving strategies. Possible options include:

   ☐ Individual retirement accounts (IRAs)

   ☐ Keogh plans

   ☐ Profit-sharing and pension plans

   ☐ Simplified Employee Pension (SEP) plans

☐ Stay abreast of current tax-saving trends by regularly meeting with your accountant, reading business magazines, and attending business tax seminars.

Strategies and Tips

 From knowing what it will cost you to open your doors to knowing how to manage your finances, preplanning is the key to helping you through the money matters aspect of the business game. It cannot be emphasized enough that you need to have a clear understanding of your financial position *before* starting your business. These checklists are just tips for getting you started down the preplanning path. Take the information you have gleaned from this chapter, and develop your Plan of Action for Money Matters on page 53.

▪ Be as conservative as possible when budgeting for your start-up expenses. Start small, and buy as you grow.

▪ Don't be surprised if a bank is unwilling to set up credit card arrangements until it knows you better. Going to a bank with your business plan, complete with projections, and explaining your business, will get you started on the right foot.

▪ If you plan to get a loan, don't even dream of going to a bank until you develop a cash-flow projection. Banks are relying on these projections more now than ever. And they will want the estimates to be backed up with supporting information and documents and reasonable estimates.

- Funding your business through partnerships or venture capitalists requires the help of a lawyer or accountant, or both. Except in very unusual circumstances, you are going to need professional help. However, if you operate as a sole proprietorship, you can use your own money without major problems from the IRS.

- Commercial banks have become increasingly more receptive over the past two decades to the financing needs of small businesses. As a result, commercial banks rank as the largest single source of extended-term financing for small businesses.

- Be honest with your banker. If you have a problem, let the banker know before the word spreads on the streets.

- If you need to borrow money for your business and cannot obtain regular bank financing, do not overlook the possibility of obtaining a loan through the U.S. Small Business Administration. While many entrepreneurs think a business must be a minority-owned one to qualify for SBA financing, this is not the case.

- Cash flow refers to how you obtain your cash, not your sales. There is a major difference between cash and credit, and how cash flows into your business will determine if you stay in business.

- A well-defined, well-written credit policy will make your future customers feel that you treat all customers equally.

- Payroll is a special accounting issue because you must prepare timely reports for the IRS and your state tax department. The lack of accuracy in your payroll records can result in fines and penalties; therefore, many small companies use outside services to compute their payroll and make these reports.

- Certain employee fringe benefits make for nice tax deductions in a business operation. In fact, as long as they are reasonable in amount, the IRS seldom raises any questions when they are deducted on a business tax return.

- Recognize that negotiating your business insurance is a never-ending process. You will negotiate before, during, and after your purchases for better prices, coverage, and service.

- Being a well-educated and informed insurance buyer puts you in control of your purchase.

Helpful Resources

Bottom Line Basics
The Oasis Press/PSI Research

Grants Pass, OR

(503) 479-9464
(800) 228-2275

With its easy-to-follow, ten-step plan of attack, this book guides you past the mechanics of accounting to an understanding of how financial management helps meet your business goals. $19.95 for paperback or $39.95 for 3-ring binder.

Business Owner's Guide to Accounting and Bookkeeping
The Oasis Press/PSI Research

Grants Pass, OR

(503) 479-9464
(800) 228-2275

This essential primer will help you interpret and prepare financial statements and organize your own set of books. $19.95.

The Buyer's Guide to Business Insurance
The Oasis Press/PSI Research

Grants Pass, OR

(503) 479-9464
(800) 228-2275

This book includes step-by-step guidance, ideas, and tips on how to improve your business insurance costs, coverage, and service from both agents and companies. This nontechnical reference guide shows you how to get the best property and casualty insurance coverage at the lowest price. $19.95.

Collection Techniques for Small Business
The Oasis Press/PSI Research

Grants Pass, OR

(503) 479-9464
(800) 228-2275

From establishing a credit policy to preparing for small claims court, you will find this book extremely helpful in avoiding bad debts and solving your collection problems. $19.95.

Financing Your Small Business
The Oasis Press/PSI Research

Grants Pass, OR

(503) 479-9464
(800) 228-2275

This book features essential techniques to successfully identify, approach, attract, and manage sources of financing. It also shows you how to gain the full benefits of debt financing while minimizing its risks. A great book for beginning business owners. $19.95.

The Insurance Assistant **Software**
The Oasis Press/PSI Research
Grants Pass, OR
(503) 479-9464
(800) 228-2275

This companion software to The Oasis Press book, *The Buyer's Guide to Business Insurance*, helps guide you through the process of filling out the book's Underwriting Information Questionnaire, which features questions covering various aspects of your business. The program also has several sample letters to help you gather insurance information easier. $29.95, includes book and software.

The Money Connection
The Oasis Press/PSI Research
Grants Pass, OR
(503) 479-9464
(800) 228-2275

This book is a listing of financing sources, such as venture capitalists, Small Business Investment Companies, and other public and private sources of funding for small businesses. Updated annually. $24.95.

National Venture Capital Association
Arlington, VA
(703) 351-5269

You can purchase a list of association members that includes names of venture capital firms, their addresses, phone numbers, and contact persons.

Raising Capital: How to Write a Financing Proposal
The Oasis Press/PSI Research
Grants Pass, OR
(503) 479-9464
(800) 228-2275

This book shows you how to write a financing proposal to secure business loans, venture capital, or grants. $19.95.

Start A Business
The Oasis Press/PSI Research
Grants Pass, OR
(503) 479-9464
(800) 228-2275

If you have an IBM/PC compatible computer, call about this software program that will make doing your personal and business financial projections much easier and quicker.

Successful Business Plan: Secrets & Strategies
The Oasis Press/PSI Research
Grants Pass, OR
(503) 479-9464
(800) 228-2275

A start-to-finish guide to creating a successful business plan. Provides insider tips on writing a business plan and handy financials to make it easier to compile your information. Templates are provided in the software kit for several of the worksheets found in the book. A standalone version is also available. $21.95 for paperback, but consider the complete business plan kit for $49.95.

Top Tax Saving Ideas for Today's Small Business
The Oasis Press/PSI Research

Grants Pass, OR
(503) 479-9464
(800) 228-2275

This layperson-friendly book takes the complex world of taxes and offers practical tax-saving solutions and strategies for the small business owner. The book covers topics such as home office expenses, tax write-offs for travel and entertainment, and how the latest tax laws will affect your future. $14.95.

Western Association of Venture Capitalists

Menlo Park, CA
(415) 854-1322

A directory of members is available for a fee. This association has more than 120 members, representing many of the most active venture capitalists west of the Rockies. The directory includes information on areas of investment interest, stages of companies funded, and contact names.

Notes

Plan of Action for Money Matters

Your company will hire an:
☐ In-house accountant ☐ Accounting consultant

Use this planning tool to organize and prioritize the activities in this chapter that you need to do to start your business. Don't feel you have to list all the activities you have checked off. You can simply start with the top ten most important ones and go from there, or do whatever is easiest for you. Be sure to make plenty of copies of this cut-out worksheet for your planning and organizing activities for this chapter.

Action to be Taken	Begin Date	Who	Deadline
_____	_____	_____	_____
_____	_____	_____	_____
_____	_____	_____	_____
_____	_____	_____	_____
_____	_____	_____	_____
_____	_____	_____	_____
_____	_____	_____	_____
_____	_____	_____	_____
_____	_____	_____	_____
_____	_____	_____	_____
_____	_____	_____	_____
_____	_____	_____	_____
_____	_____	_____	_____
_____	_____	_____	_____
_____	_____	_____	_____
_____	_____	_____	_____
_____	_____	_____	_____
_____	_____	_____	_____
_____	_____	_____	_____
_____	_____	_____	_____
_____	_____	_____	_____

Plan of Action (continued)

Action to be Taken	Begin Date	Who	Deadline

Chapter 3

Marketing Strategies

Introduction

Anyone who has played chess before knows about the concentration and strategizing a player does before she makes a move on the board. If a player makes a poor move, it may very well cost her the game. On the other hand, if a player makes a well-thought-out move and has an overall game strategy, then she may achieve checkmate and win.

When it comes to strategizing your business' marketing plan, you need to concentrate and focus on the moves you will make to get your message out to your target market effectively and create more sales and profits. You can save yourself significant amounts of money if you:

- Take the time, energy, and initial investment to carefully determine your target markets;
- Test market your product or service;
- Evaluate your tests and make modifications, if indicated; and
- Understand your advertising options and budgeting needs before you start your business.

These activities will help you avoid poor marketing efforts and increase your sales by reaching a more targeted buyer. In short, by doing an initial plan of action and completing necessary investigation and research, you will know what to anticipate in terms of developing and budgeting for a marketing plan.

Conversely, by not planning your marketing strategy, you can spend too much time and resources on the wrong marketing effort and miss possible opportunities for new markets and sales. Ultimately, you could lose a large amount of money on wasted efforts, or worse, your business could fail.

By now, you know if you will be marketing a product, service, or both, and if you will be a retailer, manufacturer, service company, or home-based business. Whichever is the case, the actions outlined in this chapter will help you learn the marketing aspects and issues to consider before starting your business. This chapter takes you through the activities necessary for initial market research, marketing communication strategies, marketing plans, and marketing budgets.

First Aid for Marketing Strategies

Most of the information and activities listed in Chapter 3 are based on a comprehensive, how-to marketing book entitled, *Power Marketing for Small Business*, written by Jody Hornor. If you need a basic, all-in-one marketing book to help you learn about marketing in general, then *Power Marketing* is the book for you. You will find this book extremely valuable in completing all of the activities mentioned in this chapter.

Another valuable marketing book you may find helpful is *Marketing Mastery: Your Seven Step Guide to Success*, written by Harriet Stephenson and Dorothy Otterson.

You can obtain a copy of these books in any local bookstore, or you could order directly from the publisher.

Marketing Mastery: Your Seven Step Guide to Success
Power Marketing for Small Business
The Oasis Press/PSI Research
Grants Pass, OR
(503) 479-9464
(800) 228-2275

Other valuable sales and marketing resources are listed at the end of this chapter. These resources could be of assistance when you formulate your Plan of Action for Marketing Strategies worksheet on page 79.

Market Research

Remember when you wrote a high school research paper or wrote a detailed analysis or report for your employer? Before you handed in the final paper, you had to roll up your sleeves and do some research on the subject or topic at hand. The same principle applies when developing a marketing strategy for your business.

With a marketing plan, you need to learn who your target market is, what that market needs and how it buys, plus you need to learn how your product or service stands out in the crowd and if it is feasible to market your product or service in a particular market segment. This all takes time and research, but don't be discouraged or daunted by the prospect of spending some time in the library, on the phone, or with an adviser. Look at it as a treasure hunt. Every bit of data and information you discover will lead you closer to your pot of gold — a successful and prosperous business.

Don't underestimate the importance of market research in your marketing strategy. Market research will help you focus on the long term and is designed to closely support both strategic marketing and product planning. Go at it with enthusiasm and focus. Use the checklists in this section to give you an idea of what you will need to do.

Target Market Checklist

Targeting your market with the use of demographic data (age, sex, income, and education) and psychographic data (lifestyle characteristics, such as hobbies, preferences, and social groups) helps you get the most out of your sales and advertising efforts because you can better target those customers who are most likely to purchase your product or service. To determine where and how you should advertise, you need to understand exactly who your prospect or potential customer is.

☐ Determine the demographic profile of the people most likely to purchase your product or service — your target market. To collect demographic data, you can use:

　☐ A survey with in-person questionnaires or conduct a survey by phone;

　☐ Private research firms;

　☐ Trade and professional associations;

　☐ U.S. Bureau of the Census data; and

　☐ U.S. Small Business Administration materials.

☐ Determine the psychographic profile of the people most likely to purchase your product or service. To collect psychographic data, you can use the options listed above. In addition, consider:

Who or what influences your target market in its buying decisions?

How does your market shop for and buy similar products or services?

Are your market's attitudes, values, or habits changing? If so, how?

☐ Write a description of your target market after you have determined its demographics and psychographics. Ask yourself these questions as you complete this aspect of your market research:

Is the product or service you offer geared to a consumer or business prospect?

Can everyone in that consumer or business group use your product, or is there a particular type of business or individual that is more apt to purchase it?

Does age, sex, income level, or lifestyle of the business or individual indicate a more qualified prospect?

☐ Divide your target market into market segments if the target market is too large for you to reach with your budget or the available marketing media.

Product or Service Checklist

Once you know who your target market is and what motivates it to buy, consider how your product or service is unique, why it is appealing, and how you can get feedback on your product or service so you know if it is feasible to go ahead with your marketing plans.

☐ List all your product or service's strengths and weaknesses.

_____

_____

_____

_____

_____

_____

_____

_____

☐ List all your product or service's physical features or aspects and all of the benefits it provides to customers.

_____

_____

_____

_____

_____

_____

☐ List all of your competitors and their strengths and weaknesses.

_____

_____

_____

_____

_____

_____

☐ Compare your product or service to those of your competitors, and assess how you stand out from the rest.

☐ Note any unique features or benefits you offer over those of your competitors so you can use this position in your marketing strategies.

☐ Create a catchy, five-to-seven word slogan that captures this position.

☐ Test market your product or service to determine its most appropriate price, packaging, shipping methods, and so on. Important questions to keep in mind:

Can you sell your product or service for a price that is profitable?

Are the attributes of your product or service desirable and saleable?

Which packaging encourages the most sales?

What constitutes a successful test market? By what criteria will you judge your results?

How are you going to track your results?

Which variable will you test first, second, third? Never test market two variables at the same time, you cannot track results.

☐ Compare your price with those of your competitors to see if it is reasonable and workable in your market.

☐ Compare your price with the price of producing the product or providing the service.

☐ Specify any guarantees or warranties you will offer.

How do they compare with your competitors?

Will they be limited guarantees or warranties?

How will a warranty affect your price?

☐ Research any buying objections your target market may have regarding your product or service.

How can you overcome these buying objections?

Will any solutions require product modifications or a change in your marketing message?

☐ Ensure your product packaging is professional and appropriate.

Does the package represent the business in the way you want it to be perceived?

Is the packaging cost-effective?

Is the packaging environment-friendly?

☐ Ensure the packaging for your service is professional and represents the company well.

Market Research Sources and Techniques

Trying to figure out where to start and how to conduct your market research for your target market and product or service can seem pretty overwhelming at first. But thanks to several leading marketing experts and consultants, there are many how-to, self-help marketing books available. *Know Your Market: How to Do Low-Cost Market Research* by David B. Frigstad is one of these helpful publications.

In his book, Mr. Frigstad explains how you can obtain primary and secondary sources of information, as well as various techniques for researching marketing and sales issues, all of which can help you either write your own marketing plan or set up your company's market information system (MIS). An MIS is when you organize procedures and methods that will gather market information on an ongoing and regular basis. A discussion of what to include in a marketing plan occurs later in this chapter.

So, to help you get out of the starting blocks and up and running with your market research — which is an extremely important role in the business game — this section features a couple of checklists that are based upon the information presented in *Know Your Market*.

Market Research Sources Checklist

When you begin your research to learn more about your target market or your particular industry, you can use either primary or secondary sources of data and information. Primary research is obtained by gathering information directly from a consumer, supplier, or competitor and is vital to any research project's completion. Secondary research, however, is aimed more at familiarizing a researcher with an industry's technology, jargon, and trends. Secondary research is used more to complement a research project rather than completing one. Secondary research can be divided into two types: internal (in-house) and external (outside the business).

☐ Before beginning any research project, outline all the details you wish to cover. For instance:

  ☐ Determine how long the forecast period will be for your various marketing aspects, including sales forecasts or technological trends.

  ☐ Decide what to include in the forecast, such as pricing considerations.

  ☐ Identify potential markets and note all product applications, including market application segments, end-user segments, and geographic segments.

  ☐ Identify the fields of technology you need to analyze.

  ☐ Consider which competitors to analyze and exactly what information you will want to gather about each one.

  ☐ Define what type of information you want regarding the end-user of your product or service.

☐ Once you know what research information you need, select which primary data collection method you will use. Primary research collection methods include:

  ☐ Mail surveys or questionnaires

  ☐ Personal interviews

  ☐ Telephone interviews

☐ Research how to effectively conduct your interviews or surveys.

    ☐ Develop the questionnaires for your survey or interview.

☐ In addition to primary sources, don't forget your internal secondary sources of information. They can include:

    ☐ Your company's projected or past sales and marketing reports; and

    ☐ Your company's projected or past accounting and financial records and statements.

☐ Gather as many external secondary sources as possible. Consider using:

    ☐ Associations pertaining to your business or trade;

    ☐ Computerized bibliographies or on-line services;

    ☐ Government agencies and publications; and

    ☐ Public library reference desks.

☐ Consider attending industry trade shows to gather preliminary market information on such topics as marketing strategies, product information, competitors, customer interest levels, and technical trends.

☐ Educate yourself on the basics of sales forecasting and how it can help you project sales figures and be a vital part of your market research.

Competitor Research Techniques Checklist

The primary goal of competitor research is to obtain an understanding of where your competitors are situated in the marketplace and to outline the likely strategic decisions a specific competitor might make. Competitive analysis should try to determine the competitor's strategy and estimate the subsequent effects, if any, on your own company.

When you write any business plan or marketing plan, you will need to include information on how you stand up or compare to your competition. In fact, several checklists throughout *Start Your Business* ask you to do this kind of analysis or research. This checklist should help you in this endeavor.

☐ Begin your competitor research by investigating your competitors in the following areas:

    ☐ Company organization

    ☐ Cost structure

    ☐ Distribution channels

    ☐ Financial position

□ Management structure and style

□ Product line

□ Research and development

□ Assess your competitors' objectives, including their financial, technical, market leadership, and general performance objectives.

□ Identify the underlying beliefs of your competition by understanding how they perceive themselves, the market in general, and their competition.

□ Focus on how your competitors operate.

What markets or niches do your competitors appear to concentrate on, and how do they compete in those markets? For example, is the competitor competing primarily on the basis of price, or is it focusing on technological differentiation of products?

□ Consider the following sources for gathering competitor information:

□ Company interviews

□ Company literature

□ End-user history

□ Government filings

□ Number of employees

□ Plant inspections

□ Visual observations

Market Analysis Techniques Checklist

When you need to take an in-depth look at your particular marketplace, you can employ several different approaches. Generally, no one market analysis technique is better than the other, and an ideal approach to this aspect of your research project would be to combine some or all of the methods mentioned in this checklist.

□ Do a preliminary sales analysis of your company by doing sales forecasting or reviewing any existing sales records.

□ Learn about the life cycle of your product or service and how each stage of the cycle will affect your price and position within your marketplace.

□ Analyze how you should price your product or service by evaluating your projected sales figures, the life cycle stage of your product or service, and your position in the marketplace.

☐ Evaluate ways you will gain a larger share of your target market.

☐ Always be researching new trends in technology that will affect your market.

Marketing Communications Strategies

With the initial market research completed on your target market and product or service, you are aware of the people you need to reach and what you need to tell them about your product or service. In addition, you know how to position your product or service against your competitors; what price is most effective; and how you will package your product or service. Now you need to ask: "How will you let your target market know about your product or service?"

To educate your target market about your product or service, you need to "talk" to your market. This is where marketing communications comes into play. It is through marketing communications — public relations, advertising, and sales — that you are able to get your message out to your target market, get its attention, and eventually get its business. As a new business owner, simply getting a feel for marketing communications is a step in the right direction. The checklists in this section will not only do this for you, but they will also make you think about details and information to incorporate into your first marketing communications strategy.

This section points out how you can utilize these marketing communications options and raise some issues and activities that will move you towards a strong marketing strategy.

Public Relations Checklist

Public relations helps you gain credibility and visibility in your market at little or no cost because instead of purchasing advertising time or space, you submit newsworthy information to the editorial side of a medium — such as a television station or newspaper — which in turn, may broadcast or publish the information.

With a minimum amount of effort and an easily learned writing ability, any small business can and is encouraged to use a public relations program in its marketing communications strategies. Here are some activities for developing a public relations program for your new business.

☐ List all the media — newspapers, radio, and television stations — in your local area, plus any other media that would be interested in your product or service.

Is there a national trade magazine that covers your industry or an out-of-state or local radio station that has a talk show applicable to your industry?

Does your local newspaper have a regular business section where you can send newsworthy information regarding your product or service?

☐ Make sure your media list includes the medium's name, a contact person, a mailing address, and a phone number. Ideally, your list should also note a medium's reach or circulation and any editorial material it reviews.

☐ Request a media kit from each of the mediums on your list. See the Glossary for a definition on media kits.

☐ From their media kits, see which of the media reaches your target market and disregard the rest.

☐ Recognize what a newsworthy event is for most media. Events, such as opening a new business, promoting an employee, or honors or awards achieved, will usually get a mention in the local media.

☐ Learn how to write an effective news release.

☐ Create a start-up public relations calendar for the first six-months of operation.

What company events or activities would be of interest to the local, regional, or national media? New hires? New product introduction? Your grand opening?

What months will these events and activities be occurring in?

☐ Designate who will write the news release, organize the mailing, and do the follow up.

☐ Join your local chamber of commerce, local business organizations, or become involved with community projects and events. Networking is a valuable part of any public relations program.

Advertising Checklist

Advertising is an integral part of any overall marketing communications strategy because you can use so many different media to get your message out to a large number of people. As a result, advertising can generate more sales and higher profits.

Depending on your product or service and your own advertising goals, you will most likely use a mix of media options to fulfill your needs. Once you have evaluated your available media options and know which ones are the most effective in reaching your target market, you can begin to develop a media strategy that works for your new business.

The checklist below helps you get a general feel for advertising and media strategies. Take your time to review each activity and begin to formulate your own media-buying strategy.

☐ Write down what messages you want your target market to hear.

_____

_____

_____

_____

 Are you unknown in the market? If so, your message may be to simply generate awareness of your product or service and establish some credibility — you do not want to close a sale by offering a discount.

☐ Ensure your advertising message recognizes both the needs of a prospective customer and the typical time frame in which he is likely to act by either purchasing or inquiring about your product or service.

 If you have a new product, it will take longer for a customer to respond. Your message shouldn't be geared towards closing a sale, but rather, it should focus on gaining the attention of your market.

☐ Once you have a clear idea of what messages to send, determine all your company's communications goals. For example:

    ☐ Create awareness of your company, product, or service.

    ☐ Educate the market about who you are and what you do.

    ☐ Position the company against a major competitor.

    ☐ Influence hidden decision makers in the buying chain.

    ☐ Generate inquiries to start the sales process.

    ☐ Generate orders to create sales.

☐ Check off the potential media sources (listed below) you would consider buying advertising from. Some of your media options include:

☐ Billboard/outdoor advertising	☐ Newspapers
☐ Cooperative advertising	☐ Radio
☐ Direct mail	☐ Signs
☐ Directories	☐ Specialty advertising
☐ Magazines	☐ Television
☐ Newsletters	☐ Yellow Pages

☐ Request a media kit from each media source you might be interested in using.

☐ Review each media kit to discover the medium's total audience reach, that audience's demographics, and what the medium charges for ads.

☐ Calculate the cost-per-qualified contact by simply dividing the number of qualified prospects the medium reaches by how much it will cost you to advertise with that medium.

☐ Make a list of all the media that most effectively reaches your target audience for the least amount of money.

Optional Media Strategies and Research Checklist

To give you a more comprehensive feel for some of the details involved in advertising, try to complete some of the activities mentioned in this section. Learn as much as possible about the media and what is available to you. The more you know, the better prepared you will be for your business' marketing needs and efforts.

The checklist below is designed to get you thinking about how you will approach working with the media.

☐ Investigate any opportunities you may have for co-op advertising.

 Do you have any regional or national suppliers that offer co-op advertising? If so, give them a call.

Would you be interested in starting your own co-op advertising?

☐ Develop a sample direct mail program to get a better feel for how economical and valuable this marketing communications strategy is for small businesses. To start:

☐ Purchase a mailing list of qualified or target customers.

☐ Decide on the type of direct mail piece you wish to send. For example:

    ☐ A post card

    ☐ A four-color piece

    ☐ A one-sheet advertisement with a discount coupon attached

☐ Estimate how much your postage will cost.

☐ Design a way to track the response of your mailer, so you can keep track of results.

☐ Research the opportunities involved in database or relationship marketing. See the Glossary for a definition.

☐ Observe how your future competitors operate.

Do their media mixes seem effective? How do they advertise? What can you learn from their strategies?

☐ Explore the option of using an advertising agency for assistance in developing an overall advertising campaign.

Can an advertising agency save you time and money because of its expertise and connections?

Is a particular agency more reputable and comparable in cost to other advertising agencies?

☐ Review industry publications and pick out ads that catch your eye. Be aware of what makes a good ad and keep examples of them in a file for future reference.

☐ Look for competitor ads in local, regional, or national newspapers and magazines. Keep a file on these ads too.

☐ Introduce yourself to a local printer to get suggestions on where to learn more about the printing business.

    ☐ Find out what type of printer you will most likely need; for example, quick printing, light commercial printing, web press printing, or large commercial printing.

    ☐ Investigate how prices are determined.

    ☐ Familiarize yourself with common printing terms such as bleeds, screens, halftones, special effects, and quantities.

    ☐ Ask about how to get print bids for advertising literature and ads.

Sales Strategies

A sales team often carries out many of the marketing strategies a company develops for itself. Salespeople communicate with a market through a variety of marketing communications methods, such as telemarketing, in-person sales presentations, and direct mail. If you decide to have a sales team in your new venture, which sales methods your team will use depends on your general sales department's goals and your type of business. Even if you don't plan on having a sales team on staff when you open your doors, quickly review the checklists that follow so you can be better informed and knowledgeable about what you will need to think through and decide on once you realize a sales department will be necessary for your business to remain competitive and successful. Don't make the wrong move when it comes to knowing all your sales strategy options!

General Sales Department Goals Checklist

To streamline your in-house operations and satisfy your customers, communications between your sales department and all your business' other departments is critical. The exchange of customer feedback and data with that of production schedules, shipping and receiving guidelines, order entry procedures, and customer account situations ensures your sales department will be more effective. To have clear communications, think about some general goals for your sales department. Review the checklist below for some ideas.

☐ Define the role of sales in your marketing strategy.

Will you need a sales team to begin your operations, or do you anticipate the need for a sales team later on?

What sales strategies can your sales team use to help carry out your overall marketing communications strategy?

Will you rely on media to increase sales or will you do in-person sales calls?

☐ Consider your sales staffing options:

☐ An in-house staff

☐ Representative firms — see the Glossary for definition.

☐ Direct sales — no sales staff necessary because mail piece or advertisement becomes salesperson.

☐ Do-it-yourself

☐ If an in-house staff is desired, you will need to set up a process to:

    ☐ Recruit, select, and hire qualified team players.

    ☐ Educate them on your product or service.

    ☐ Train them on how to sell your product or service.

    ☐ Determine sales territories, if necessary.

    ☐ Develop compensation programs for the sales team.

    ☐ Motivate, evaluate, and measure performance.

☐ Identify key customer accounts and develop sales strategies that will help close a sale quickly and efficiently.

☐ Determine how often you will meet with your sales team, and develop a schedule of regular meetings to ask your salespeople for customer feedback and data. Let them know about:

    ☐ Upcoming advertising campaigns, such as a direct mail piece or an ad in a local newspaper.

    ☐ Any existing problems in production or manufacturing that will affect product deadlines and promised delivery dates.

    ☐ Increases or decreases in the cost of any of your products or services, including temporary discount offers or permanent increases.

    ☐ Accounting problems with a particular customer.

Direct Sales Strategies Checklist

Playing the business game means getting out and meeting with the players one on one. As a result, one of the most common ways a business communicates with its prospective customers is through direct sales.

Here is a checklist on what you can do to start your one-on-one sales strategies.

☐ Ensure you and your sales team are always very professional in appearance. Be well-groomed and appropriately dressed.

☐ Choose how you will make your sales calls.

    ☐ By telephone (telemarketing)

    ☐ Direct mail piece

    ☐ In-person

    ☐ Video

☐ Examine and refine your sales presentation.

How will you greet or introduce yourself to prospects?

How do you want to present or inform the prospect about your product or service?

What are your product's attributes or your service's unique aspects? Would you want to emphasize these in your presentation?

☐ Create a friendly, professional sales environment for your customers, whether it is a retail store, your home or business office, or a third-party setting, such as a restaurant.

☐ Develop a policy on customer service.

Will you take the extra steps necessary to help someone, even though it is clear she will not purchase from you immediately?

Will you give free how-to advice if it means possibly losing a sale or opportunity to perform your service at that time?

What kind of return policy will you offer?

Will you or your employees refer customers to competitors, if you do not have what the customer needs?

☐ Develop an effective, follow-up system for customer inquiries that will help ensure customer satisfaction and inspire referrals.

    ☐ Create informational sales literature on each of your products or services so you have some material on hand when needed.

    ☐ Keep track of who makes inquiries and make sure you develop a process that ensures follow up within 48 hours of an inquiry.

Other Sales Strategy Factors Checklist

In addition to all the activities mentioned above, you may also want to explore some other factors involved in creating a strong sales strategy for your new business. Review the checklist below to gather ideas that may apply to your new address.

☐ Help close a sale faster by advertising often to your target market before sending in your sales team.

☐ Investigate what trade shows may benefit your business and consider attending them.

☐ Use testimonials from existing customers to encourage more sales and provide more credibility.

☐ Consider working with a trade or professional association to help sell your product or service to its membership. (See the *NTPA Directory* for a good source of possible associations. For information on getting this directory, refer to Helpful Resources at the end of this chapter.)

☐ Have product videos do the talking for you. Observe how other businesses utilize video in their sales strategies and see if it is a medium applicable for your new business.

☐ Network with related or complementary businesses to refer customers back and forth.

☐ Ensure the price you are asking conveys a positive product image. For example, don't have a price that is so low, it conveys inferior quality.

☐ Evaluate how you will distribute your product and how that distribution channel will affect your sales and marketing strategies.

Is your distribution channel feasible? Does it meet market needs and wants? Is it reliable? Does it deliver fast enough for the customers? How much will it cost?

Is your distribution channel profitable? Consider how many middlepeople there will be, how much advertising will be within that channel, and how the channel will affect your product packaging and shipping.

☐ If you are considering mail order as a distribution channel, know the Federal Trade Commission rules and regulations regarding mail order, plus those for your state of residence.

Marketing Plans

Writing a marketing plan is much like writing a game plan for a particular sport. The business owner and sports coach alike are both detailing goals, procedures, and methods that will help them achieve their ultimate goal of winning the game!

By writing down the specifics of a marketing plan, you can clearly indicate how to accomplish your company's marketing goals in an efficient manner. Don't be intimidated by this endeavor. It will require substantial research, but with the checklists below and the checklists featured in the Market Research Sources and Techniques section on page 60, you will know what and how to research, and how to organize your findings into a readable, useful marketing plan.

Marketing Plan Components Checklist

How long or short your marketing plan will be depends on the scope of your research and the amount of detail you want to include in your plan. Regardless of length, your marketing plan should contain most, if not all, of the information mentioned in the checklist below.

☐ Write an introduction for your marketing plan.

 What is your purpose behind writing the plan?

What products or services are you selling?

What states do you sell your products or services in?

☐ Include a section on your product or service.

   ☐ Specify where it is used, how it is used, and why it is needed.

☐ List your specific goals and objectives for your new business.

☐ Do an external evaluation of your marketplace. Include:

   ☐ Any assumptions about the marketplace you are making that could affect your goals and objectives;

   ☐ The size and type of your market; and

   ☐ The strengths and weaknesses of your competitors.

☐ Do an internal evaluation of your marketplace. Include:

   ☐ A sales forecast of the first three years of business;

   ☐ A list of your company's strengths and weaknesses in the market;

   ☐ An analysis of how you are positioned in the market; and

   ☐ An analysis of how you expect to do financially in the first years of operation.

☐ Discuss your overall marketing strategy for your business. Consider:

 What needs to happen before any of your sales forecasts become a reality?

What are the changing and current trends in your marketplace?

How do you propose to reach your customers? What is your media mix and how much sales revenue do you anticipate will be necessary for you to break even on your advertising?

☐ Prepare a financial summary to help you see if your marketing strategy and plan will work at a profit.

- ☐ Try to cover gross margins, sales and marketing expenses, investment requirements, and returns on investments.

- ☐ Have your accountant review your predictions and provide advice on layout and figures.

Marketing Budgets

You probably wouldn't consider financing a new car or computer without first looking at your income and expenses to see if such a purchase was affordable. Likewise, you don't want to buy advertising time, create sales literature, or hire a complete staff of salespeople without first researching your business' potential sales figures and anticipated marketing expenses.

Because many new start ups have a limited amount of capital and funding, most new business owners use their own money for advertising and marketing budgets. As a result, many such budgets are often small to start off with, but they usually increase as effective strategies are employed and sales begin to increase.

Take the time to review the checklists in this section so you are more familiar with the marketing budget process. See if you can come up with a marketing budget based on your own forecasting and budgeting experience.

Budgeting Basics Checklist

If you are like many new entrepreneurs, the financial end of your business may seem intimidating and one you would rather not deal with directly. Regardless of whether or not you will have an accountant do all your financial statements and bookkeeping, it makes good business sense to, at a minimum, have a basic understanding of the factors that go into budgeting. The checklist featured below includes a couple of budgeting basics you can think about when formulating your marketing budget.

Refer to Chapter 2 for more checklists and information regarding financial issues.

- ☐ Forecast the total sales figure you anticipate for the first year of operation. Consider factors that will most likely increase sales in your first year.

 Will you be increasing your advertising?

Will you be developing more marketing strategies?

Will you be hiring salespeople?

☐ Calculate the costs you anticipate for the implementation of your marketing strategies.

  ☐ Review trade and professional publications for information on average business expenses in your industry.

  ☐ Ask other business owners how they operate, the costs involved, and any advice they can give on budgeting for marketing expenses.

  ☐ Study your competitors' advertising expenditures.

    Because you are starting a new business, you will have to anticipate spending a lot of time and money educating your market about your product or service through advertising and public relations.

☐ Look hard for any and all data to help you budget your marketing dollars.

☐ Study target markets and media options to determine where to best spend your marketing dollars.

Strategies and Tips

Nearly all new businesses will have to rely on a good marketing strategy in order to succeed in their marketplaces. If you have completed checking off the applicable activities listed in this chapter's checklists, you are off to a good start in achieving this goal. Review the extra tips and sources in the information provided below to augment your initial marketing plan of action.

- Without research, you can't position against or differentiate your product or service from your competitors, and lack of differentiation in the marketplace translates into reasons why many businesses fail.

- Use secondary research data before and during the primary research phase to identify potential primary sources and gain improved insight into the research problem or project.

- Many small businesses have a tendency to set up shop and take anyone as a customer or offer any product or service simply so they can get business. In the long run, this has not proved to be a useful or profitable strategy. A small business needs to target its products and services to a qualified market so the business gets the most for its marketing dollar.

- Your goal is to buy media advertising that reaches the most qualified prospects for the lowest cost.

- If you have trouble deciding where you should advertise, you may wish to pursue the services of an advertising agency or a good freelance advertising or marketing consultant. The fees they charge may be worth the time you save in research and decision making.

- At all costs, be professional in your advertising. Make sure your printed ads are error free, well balanced, and visually pleasing.

- Companies that are new to the marketplace will ordinarily have to spend more for advertising than their established counterparts.

- Studies show that most sales are made after nine advertising exposures to a product or service, and only every third media exposure gets seen by prospects.

- Direct sales, as well as other advertising, will persist where salespeople don't. Several studies of outside selling activities indicate that more than 80 percent of all sales are made after the fifth sales call, but only 10 percent of the salespeople studied persisted that long.

- The customer feedback the salespeople receive every day from talking with the marketplace is valuable information that can help you keep on top of customer needs and wants, not to mention ways of keeping your product or service competitive and unique.

- Not only are trade shows a good place to meet prospective buyers, they are also good sources of market information when conducting market research.

- A sales forecasting rule of thumb: Prepare realistic projections. Triple your expenses. Halve your sales numbers. Then use the forecast.

Helpful Resources

A Business Guide to the Federal Trade Commission's Mail Order Rule
Federal Trade Commission
Washington, DC
(202) 326-2222

A free publication available to anyone interested in learning about the FTC Mail Order Rule. Very helpful in answering basic questions about the rule.

Customer Engineering: Cutting Edge Selling Strategies
The Oasis Press/PSI Research
Grants Pass, OR
(503) 479-9464
(800) 228-2275

This book discusses the customer engineering process, which includes analyzing your customers, developing a customer database, generating sales leads, and setting up a direct sales force, so you can determine how to increase sales and reduce costs. $19.95 for paperback or $39.95 for 3-ring binder.

Export Now
The Oasis Press/PSI Research
Grants Pass, OR
(503) 479-9464
(800) 228-2275

An excellent resource for learning about distribution channels and the way you can sell your product or service internationally. Easy-to-read text with handy appendices containing government agency information. $19.95.

How to Develop Successful Sales Promotions
American Management Association (AMA)
New York, NY
(518) 891-5510

Minimize your sales promotion risks and maximize your chances of success by applying the knowledge, techniques, and skills you get from this course book. $130.00 (A discount is available for AMA members.)

Know Your Market: How to Do Low-Cost Market Research
The Oasis Press/PSI Research
Grants Pass, OR
(503) 479-9464
(800) 228-2275

This workbook explains how a small business can conduct its own market research by providing information on practical marketing tools and techniques. $19.95.

Mail Order Legal Guide
The Oasis Press/PSI Research
Grants Pass, OR
(503) 479-9464
(800) 228-2275

Mail Order Legal Guide (continued)

For companies that use the mail to market their products or services, as well as for mail order businesses, this book clarifies complex regulations so penalties can be avoided. Gives state-by-state legal requirements, plus information on Federal Trade Commission guidelines and rules covering delivery dates, advertising, sales taxes, unfair trade practices, and consumer protection. $45.00 for 3-ring binder or $29.95 for paperback.

Marketing Mastery: Your Seven Step Guide to Success
The Oasis Press/PSI Research
Grants Pass, OR
(503) 479-9464
(800) 228-2275

This book is very helpful for the beginning marketer looking for information on how to launch a new product, create an effective marketing strategy, and retain a core of satisfied-plus customers. $19.95.

National Trade and Professional Association Directory
Columbia Books
Washington, DC
(202) 898-0662

The *National Trade and Professional Association (NTPA) Directory*, which is published by Columbia Books, is helpful in locating industry sources for the purpose of doing secondary market research, locating mailing lists, or developing media or public relations mailing lists. Call the above number for price and delivery charges regarding the directory.

Power Marketing for Small Business
The Oasis Press/PSI Research
Grants Pass, OR
(503) 479-9464
(800) 228-2275

A hands-on, easy-to-read book that details all aspects of marketing. Its user-friendly worksheets reinforce the concepts and topics discussed in the text. A great resource for the beginning marketer! $19.95 for paperback or $39.95 for 3-ring binder.

The Successful Referral Prospecting Program
Leadership Development Associates
Irvine, CA
(714) 253-4664

A step-by-step publication that guides you through the development and management of productive referral management. A comprehensive, friendly text that will help you (and your sales team) increase sales and referrals. Call for more information.

U.S. Department of Commerce
Washington, DC
(202) 482-2000

If you are looking for various publications or programs on economic development, call the above number.

Plan of Action for Marketing Strategies

Your company will market products or services as a:
☐ Retailer ☐ Wholesaler ☐ Manufacturer ☐ Service company

Use this planning tool to organize and prioritize the activities in this chapter that you need to do to start your business. Don't feel you have to list all the activities you have checked off. You can simply start with the top ten most important ones and go from there, or do whatever is easiest for you. Be sure to make plenty of copies of this cut-out worksheet for your planning and organizing activities for this chapter.

Action to be Taken	Begin Date	Who	Deadline

Plan of Action (continued)

Action to be Taken	Begin Date	Who	Deadline

Chapter 4

If Your Business Will Have Employees

Introduction

Many new start ups begin as one-person operations, but as sales increase and the businesses grow, they must look to other personnel to coordinate and support the increasing workloads.

When you hire employees, the rules of the business game thicken somewhat. In particular, you will need to be aware of the heavy amount of federal regulations that will mandate and affect your actions and communications with your future employees. From guidelines on what you can and cannot ask during an employee interview to regulations for on-the-job safety, you need to ensure you comply with both state and federal employer laws. Keep in mind these regulations are a part of the government's effort to ensure equality and fairness in employee hiring and working conditions; it is not an attempt to control you or your business, even though you may feel that way at times.

Even if you will be hiring just one employee, you will need to know the areas outlined in this chapter. This chapter's checklists help you recognize the initial processes for staffing your business, the laws and filings you will need to understand before you hire your employees, and some of the personnel paperwork you should anticipate.

Remember you are not considered an employee of your sole proprietorship or partnership. Anyone else working for your business — with the possible exception of your spouse or child — will be considered an employee. In addition, the requirements outlined in this chapter are for any type of business, regardless of its legal form or whether it is a retail, manufacturing, wholesale, service, or construction company.

First Aid for Hiring Employees

People Investment: Making Your Hiring Decisions Pay Off for Everyone is a handy book source for detailing and expanding upon the activities outlined under the following Staffing Your Business section. Both *People Investment*, as well as an informative book called *Starting and Operating a Business in . . .* (your state's name), are two good resources for dealing with the legal considerations of an employer and potential paperwork you need to perform before and after hiring your employees. For more information on these resources, contact the publisher at the toll-free number listed below.

People Investment
***Starting and Operating a Business in . . .* series**
The Oasis Press/PSI Research
Grants Pass, OR
(503) 479-9464
(800) 228-2275

In addition, you will find a number of other helpful resources located at the end of this chapter. Ranging from helpful government agencies to various publications, the Helpful Resources section will make being the captain of your own team easier.

Staffing Your Business

Assuming you will not be having an outside employment agency do the recruiting and hiring of your employees, you will have to organize a thorough, well-thought-out hiring procedure to staff your own business. This staffing procedure will take you from the creation of job descriptions to the orientation and training of the individuals you end up hiring.

By taking the time to evaluate the hiring processes now, you will be better prepared personally and financially once you begin to hire employees. You will also reduce confusion and misunderstandings because of this initial preplanning. By completing the activities featured in the checklists for this section, you will have a solid beginning for an in-house hiring and staffing procedure.

Initial Definitions Checklist

The first step for any future employer is to recruit and hire qualified individuals for specific, well-defined job positions. To accomplish this primary goal, you first must write down some initial position definitions and goals. Follow the steps below to help ensure a successful staffing procedure.

☐ List all the job positions you will need to fill before opening your doors. Your descriptions should include items, such as:

  ☐ Job titles;

  ☐ Job duties; for example, describe the everyday activities and functions of the position;

  ☐ Job requirements; for example, descriptions of the necessary tasks and the necessary tools and equipment for a particular job;

  ☐ Employee qualifications; for example, past experience, education, and special licenses;

  ☐ Wage and salary information; for example, determine what is considered a fair wage or salary for a particular job position by conducting an informal survey of other businesses or colleagues; and

  ☐ Benefits; for example, medical insurance, holiday pay, sick leave, and retirement plans.

Recruiting and Selecting Checklist

Finding the right person for any job within your new start up is crucial because you want to ensure your employees are competent, professional, and enthusiastic about their new positions so your prospective customers feel confident and satisfied about their relationship with your new business. To find these qualified individuals, review the checklist below.

☐ Prepare application forms.

  ☐ Create a separate consent form that allows you to contact an applicant's previous employers.

  ☐ Ensure you do not violate anti-discrimination laws when developing personnel questionnaires and application forms. Only ask questions related to skills needed to perform the job.

☐ Determine how you will advertise your available positions.

    ☐ Informal recruiting, such as through business associates, friends, and community resources;

    ☐ Newspaper ads;

    ☐ Magazine ads;

    ☐ Through private employment agencies;

    ☐ Through state employment services; or

    ☐ Through university or community college campus career centers.

☐ Sift through all returned application forms and compare how each applicant measures up to the job requirements.

☐ Let each applicant know you have received his application and the status of the selection process.

☐ Screen out those applicants that do not meet your minimum job qualifications.

☐ Rank the remaining applications in the priority of best qualified first and then downwards from there.

☐ Contact those applicants who are going to be interviewed for the position.

☐ Determine if you will conduct informal or formal interviews.

☐ Prepare all your questions beforehand.

☐ Ensure you will comply with state and federal anti-discrimination laws when asking interview questions. Avoid questions pertaining to:

    ☐ Dates of educational background;

    ☐ Age, race, or color;

    ☐ Sexual preference;

    ☐ Marital status;

    ☐ Religion;

    ☐ Credit status;

    ☐ Medical background, health, disability, or physical condition; and

    ☐ Child care responsibilities.

☐ Interview your top five to ten candidates for the position.

☐ Make notes immediately after each interview to ensure you write down important comments and thoughts regarding each applicant.

☐ Review your notes, carefully evaluating both the good and bad points of the interview session.

☐ Do a reference check of any applicant you are considering hiring.

    ☐ Check with your state's labor department to obtain guidance on what pre-employment information you can legally request from previous employers or personal references.

☐ If necessary or desired, test the abilities and skills (which are necessary for doing the job) of your final applicants. Definitions of the following types of tests you can use are mentioned in the Glossary:

    ☐ Achievement tests

    ☐ Aptitude tests

    ☐ Personality tests

    ☐ Situational tests

    ☐ Vocational tests[1]

☐ Present the job offer to your top candidate.

    ☐ Be clear about what is negotiable and what is not to avoid misunderstandings.

    ☐ Clarify conditions of employment.

☐ Obtain a final answer from your top candidate before contacting your other final applicants.

☐ If yes, then notify all other final applicants the position has been filled.

Training and Orientation Checklist

After you have hired your new employees, you are ready to train and orient them so their transition into your business is as smooth and as comfortable as possible. Taking the time now to formulate training and orientation strategies will only make this task easier once you have employees. Review the checklist below to help you create a basic training and orientation procedure.

☐ Have the new employee fill in necessary paperwork. See Personnel Recordkeeping Checklist on page 95.

---

1. As the owner, you cannot simply make up a test and administer it. On the contrary, any test evaluation you use on your applicants or employees must have proven itself as a sound and fair way to test individual skills properly.

☐ Take the new employee on a tour of the business' facilities.

    ☐ Introduce employees to one another.

    ☐ Explain overall operations so the new employee gets the big picture.

    ☐ Point out break areas, restrooms, or nearby locations for lunch breaks.

    ☐ Provide an informal history of the business as you go through your initial tour.

☐ Provide the employee with an employee handbook. See Company Policy Manual Checklist on page 96.

☐ Explain the purpose and function of the employee's workstation.

☐ Describe the chain of command, work relationships, and who the employee should go to with questions about the job.

☐ Briefly explain the relationship of the employee's department to other departments.

☐ Review the new employee's particular job.

☐ Ensure that the employee knows who her immediate supervisor is.

☐ Briefly explain the purpose of the job.

☐ Briefly explain the training period, how long it will last, and what is involved.

☐ Develop an initial training process for the new employee.

    ☐ Decide who will train the employee.

    ☐ Determine the length of time of the training period.

    ☐ Figure the costs involved in the training; for example, the wages of the trainer or the tuition for specialized classroom training.

    ☐ Evaluate the training process to track progress and productivity.

☐ In addition to the above initial employee training procedure, consider developing a training program to address:

    ☐ Companywide needs, such as workplace safety, use of equipment, or employee understanding of the benefits and attributes of each product or service.

    ☐ Individual employee needs, such as career advancement through in-house promotion, personal and professional growth through continued education, or professional challenges through change in responsibility or workload.

Other Staffing Options Checklist

If you don't think you will need to hire full-time, permanent help when starting your new business, but you do anticipate the need for some extra help occasionally, then you may want to explore the staffing options listed below. These options can save you a significant amount of time and money, especially when dealing with employer-related paperwork and payroll taxes.

Be aware, however, that each of these options must be carefully investigated so you don't unknowingly treat an individual as an employee for tax purposes. Definitions of these options are listed in the Glossary.

☐ Research the option of using temporary employees from an established temporary employment agency.

Are there any temporary employment agencies in your area you could call to get more information on how their operations work?

Is the temp agency licensed by the state?

What types of temps does the agency have available?

How do you go about contracting services with the temp agency?

☐ Farm out work to independent contractors.

  ☐ Contact the Internal Revenue Service (IRS) for its definition and qualifications regarding independent contractors versus employees for tax treatment purposes.

  ☐ Contact your state tax and labor departments for any guidelines on how they view independent contractors versus employees.

☐ Consider leasing employees through an established leasing company.

  ☐ Contact the state controller's office or attorney general to find out what controls, if any, the state has over employee leasing services.

Miscellaneous Staffing Activities Checklist

The activities outlined below are some of the ones you should try to consider completing before hiring employees. By taking a look at some of these issues at this time, you will streamline your personnel procedures and goals for the future and make a positive first impression on your new staff.

In addition, each of these activities should be a part of your company policy manual and employee handbook. Your findings here can be easily included in your manual and handbook. Refer to the the Company Policy Manual Checklist for more information.

☐ Develop a voluntary affirmative action program. See the Glossary for a definition.

    ☐ Contact your local Equal Employment Opportunity Commission (EEOC) office for information on how to do this.

☐ Forecast initial and long-term staffing requirements.

In what areas do you need the most employees in order to start up?

What departments or positions do you see as growing the quickest?

How many additional sales will be needed to support the hiring of new employees?

☐ Develop a salary schedule.

What will be the starting wages or salaries for each position in your business?

What will be the highest wage or salary for each position in your business?

By what criteria will increases in wages or salaries be awarded? Strictly by job performance, by length of service, or by supervisor recommendation? Or what about a combination of these qualifiers?

How will your business pay or adjust for these increases in wages or salaries?

☐ Prepare and develop an employee evaluation system. Consider:

How will you evaluate employee job performance?

Who will be responsible for reviewing employees?

How often will you do employee reviews?

Will review results be linked in any way to wage or salary increases?

☐ Decide if your business will be able to offer an employee retirement plan. If it will, you will need to:

    ☐ Comply with the Employee Retirement Income Security Act of 1974 (ERISA).

    ☐ Enlist the help of an attorney to coordinate your responsibilities under ERISA.

☐ Determine discretionary benefits, such as how your company will deal with paid vacation, sick pay, parental leave, educational assistance, and day care — to name a few.

☐ Develop procedures for promoting and terminating employees.

☐ Determine how you will deal with reducing your staff, if the situation should warrant it.

☐ Evaluate advantages and disadvantages of allowing flexible work schedules for employees.

How important is it in terms of serving the clients to have a flexible work schedule?

How does a flexible work schedule, if desired, affect the communications and coordination of work or tasks among staff members?

What are the additional financial costs of having a flexible work schedule?

What is the effect of a flexible work schedule on your ability to supervise and evaluate the performance of staff members?

Government Regulations and Taxes for Employers

Not only does the government have rules and regulations about hiring and staffing procedures that you must follow, such as equal opportunity and anti-discrimination laws, it also has a myriad of laws that specifically cover the employer-employee relationship. The checklists in this section attempt to cover the laws, registrations, filings, and taxes you must deal with once you hire your first employee. Take care to review these items very carefully. The business game can get a little complicated at this point.

Whenever possible throughout this section, the government agency that handles a particular regulation or requirement is listed in parentheses, or mentioned in the checklist activity itself, so you have an idea of where to go for more information and details. Most of these agencies' addresses and phone numbers are listed in the Helpful Resources section at the end of this chapter.

You will find two comprehensive checklists in this section: one on federal regulations and taxes and the other on state and local regulations and taxes.

Federal Employer Regulations and Taxes Checklist

This checklist includes the U.S. government's laws and acts that cover employees. Some of the acts and laws may or may not apply to your business; however, it is your responsibility to determine which ones will and won't apply. This checklist will at least give you a starting point and help you keep track of what you need to know.

☐ Apply for a federal employer identification number (EIN) by requesting *Form SS-4, Application for Employer Identification Number.* (Your local IRS office)

☐ Research the requirements outlined in the Americans with Disabilities Act of 1990 (ADA). (Your local EEOC office or the U.S. Department of Justice in Washington, D.C.)

☐ Learn about the federal Family and Medical Leave Act of 1993 to see if your new business is covered under its qualifiers. (U.S. Department of Labor)

☐ Comply with ERISA requirements if offering employees fringe benefits, such as pension plans, welfare plan benefits, or profit-sharing plans. (IRS or the U.S. Department of Labor)

☐ Know how the federal requirements of the Occupational Safety and Health Act of 1970 (OSHA) will affect your workplace safety procedures and programs.

   ☐ Contact your local federal OSHA office (or state equivalent) and request a free consultation of what OSHA standards your business needs to be aware of before opening its doors. Some basic federal OSHA requirements include:

      ☐ Posting a permanent notice to employees regarding job safety in the workplace.

      ☐ Keeping a log of all job-related injuries and illnesses on federal *Form 200.*

☐ Obtain a copy of the Fair Labor and Standards Act (FLSA) from the U.S. Department of Labor and review the federal requirements for:

   ☐ Child labor laws

   ☐ Minimum wage

   ☐ Overtime pay

   ☐ Rest periods and meal breaks

☐ Familiarize yourself with the following federal anti-discrimination laws by contacting the EEOC office nearest you. Only a few of these laws may apply to you as a start up, but learn about them for possible future application:

- [ ] Title VII of the Civil Rights Act of 1964
- [ ] Pregnancy Discrimination Act
- [ ] Executive Order 11246
- [ ] Equal Pay Act of 1963
- [ ] Age Discrimination in Employment Act of 1967
- [ ] Rehabilitation Act of 1973
- [ ] Vietnam-Era Veteran Readjustment Assistance Act of 1974
- [ ] Veterans Reemployment Rights Act of 1994

- [ ] Learn about your potential liability for sexual harassment in the workplace.

What is sexual harassment?

What types of harassment are there, and how has the EEOC dealt with them in the past?

- [ ] Obtain a copy of the Immigration Reform and Control Act of 1986 (IRCA). (U.S. Immigration and Naturalization Service – INS)

- [ ] Get several copies of *Form I-9, Employment Eligibility Verification*, from the INS.

  - [ ] Be sure all your employees fill out this form; it is a federal requirement.

  - [ ] Make a separate personnel file for I-9 forms. You don't want to file I-9 forms with regular personnel files because the federal government can demand to see I-9 forms at any time, and you don't want them to have access to your other personnel paperwork as well.

- [ ] Be prepared to withhold the following federal taxes from your employee's wages:

  - [ ] Income tax

  - [ ] Social Security (FICA) tax

- [ ] In addition, as an employer, you will be required to pay:

  - [ ] Social Security (FICA) tax; and

  - [ ] Federal unemployment tax (FUTA), if you pay wages of more than $1,500 or more during a calendar year or if one or more employees work at least a portion of the day during 20 different calendar weeks during the year.

☐ Be prepared to furnish all new employees with *Form W-4, Withholding Allowance Certificate*.

    ☐ Get copies of *Form W-4* from your local IRS office.

    ☐ Have each employee complete and return *Form W-4* to you.

    ☐ At the end of each year, furnish each employee with copies of *Form W-2, Annual Wage and Tax Statement*, showing taxable wages paid during the preceding calendar year and the tax withheld.

☐ Note: for any independent contractor you employ during a calendar year, and to whom you pay more than $600 to in compensation, you must file *Form 1099-MISC* with the IRS.

State (and Local) Employer Regulations and Taxes Checklist

In addition to the federal regulations and taxes mentioned in the above checklist, state and local governments have their own sets of laws and taxes that you need to be aware of as an employer. Employer requirements and taxes vary from state to state and from city to city.

Your best bet for knowing your state-specific employer laws is to contact your state's economic development department or one-stop business center and request a business kit of information for start-up employers. You could also contact the various agencies within the appropriate labor department in your state.

Local employer requirements can be researched through your local city hall or county clerk's office. Use the checklist below as a guide in your state-specific research.

☐ Register as an employer with the appropriate state agencies, for example, the employment division and the revenue department.

☐ Research any state-mandated family leave law that may apply to your business. (Many states have family leave laws that cover employers not covered by the federal law.)

☐ See if your state requires a workers' compensation insurance for employees — nearly all states do — and investigate how to go about obtaining this insurance.

    Is there a state-run workers' compensation insurance carrier?

    How much will this insurance cost you? For example, will you be able to join a group policy that offers reduced rates and premiums?

    How can you reduce this insurance cost?

☐ Request information from your state's occupational safety and health department and see if you need to:

  ☐ Make any filings or reports with them;

  ☐ Display any state safety posters;

  ☐ Comply with any safety standards beyond those required by federal OSHA;

  ☐ Take advantage of any free, on-site consultative programs that might be available for state employers; and

  ☐ Complete a written safety program and create a safety committee, if required.

☐ Investigate state wage-hour laws to see if any go beyond what is required of federal FLSA requirements. Don't forget to check on:

  ☐ Child labor laws;

  ☐ Minimum wage requirements and how they apply to covered employees, student workers, and disabled workers;

  ☐ Overtime pay;

  ☐ Pay period minimums;

  ☐ Rest periods and meal breaks; and

  ☐ Right-to-work laws.

☐ Compare state anti-discrimination laws with federal anti-discrimination laws to pinpoint any major differences.

☐ Withhold these state taxes from your employee's wages, if applicable:

  ☐ Income tax

  ☐ State disability insurance

☐ In addition, as an employer, you may be required to pay a state unemployment tax or workers' compensation insurance tax.

  ☐ Contact your state labor department or economic development department for more specifics on rates and other potential employer taxes.

☐ Research how to make employer tax payments and to which departments.

What forms will you need?

What is the payment schedule or deadline?

How do you figure the taxes?

☐ Determine how independent contractor payments are recorded and filed for your state.

☐ Contact all labor-related state agencies to ensure you have all the required posters for issues regarding minimum wage, child labor, overtime, unemployment benefits, and others.

☐ Contact your county clerk's office to research any applicable employer requirements for local government.

☐ Check with your local fire department to ensure you comply with fire code and safety standards for your workplace.

Personnel Paperwork

As you can imagine, all the paperwork generated by hiring employees and ensuring compliance with the numerous employer regulations can add up quickly. If you don't have a system for organizing all of these materials, you could find yourself in an office management nightmare, not knowing when you hired someone, when that person quit, or if she received the required *Form W-2* at the end of the calendar year. In addition, if you fail to keep accurate records on such things as tax payments, required filings, and OSHA procedures, you could be setting yourself up for some hefty penalties. You need to ensure your personnel files are organized and maintained efficiently.

Besides maintaining your personnel files, another form of initial paperwork is the development of your company's personnel policy manual. The minute you hire new employees, you need to clarify for them, in writing, the policies they will need and want to know about before starting their first day on the job.

Policies, such as business hours, paid vacation, sick pay, break periods, pay periods, and fringe benefits, are some of the more immediate policies new employees are interested in; however, many other policies need to be clarified as well. Policies, such as smoking rules, employee safety, performance review, dress code, and sexual harassment, are only a few of the policies you can consider including in your policy manual.

Depending on your type of business, your policies can vary in number and specifics. Developing a company policy manual before hiring your first employee will help ensure clearer communications with your staff, provide a framework for consistency and fairness, and set forth written guidelines for human resource decisions. Preventing personnel problems before they occur is important to smooth business operations and doing so usually saves time and money in the long run.

Review the checklists in this section for an overview of personnel recordkeeping and company policy manuals.

Personnel Recordkeeping Checklist

Knowing what personnel records to keep and how to organize and maintain them is crucial in the business game. Without strong recordkeeping procedures, you don't have a convenient, quick-read history of your team players or what activities you have or have not done on their behalf. You also won't have the information required by the government. Review the checklist below so you have a better idea of your recordkeeping requirements.

☐ Ensure each employee's personnel file includes the following:

☐ A completed company application form;

☐ A copy of the job description;

☐ Additional application materials, such as letters of reference or college transcripts;

☐ Emergency contact information;

☐ Pre-employment job-related test results, if given;

☐ Selection findings, if formalized;

☐ Employment contract or agreement, if used;

☐ A completed *Form W-4*;

☐ Any required state taxation forms;

☐ Payroll authorization form;

☐ Federal unemployment tax (FUTA) information;

☐ Records of wages and taxes;

☐ Records of hours worked;

☐ Records of employment history with the company; and

☐ Records of performance.

☐ Keep any medical records separate from personnel files.

☐ Know the laws pertaining to what you can and cannot have in the medical files.

Company Policy Manual Checklist

A company policy manual is your first step toward establishing written guidelines for employer-employee communications. From your policy manual, you can write your employee handbook. See the Glossary for the definitions of each.

Review the checklist below to get an idea of a policy manual outline and what to do to ensure accuracy and efficiency.

A Company Policy & Personnel Workbook is particularly helpful for the new start up creating and developing its first manual. See Helpful Resources at the end of this chapter for more information on this and other resources.

- ☐ As a general outline, have your company policy manual contain the following information:
    - ☐ Benefits
    - ☐ Career opportunities
    - ☐ Company background
    - ☐ Employee evaluation procedures
    - ☐ Employee grievance procedures
    - ☐ Employee rules and regulations
    - ☐ Employee safety
    - ☐ Employee/management relations
    - ☐ General policies and procedures
    - ☐ Pay rates and schedules

- ☐ Explain the company's policy on smoking, sexual harassment, and employee privacy.

- ☐ Have your attorney review your policy manual to ensure accuracy with all applicable business and employer laws.

- ☐ Establish a review and updating procedure for the manual.

- ☐ Create an employee handbook from your company policy manual, if desired.

Strategies and Tips

Hiring employees is always a big undertaking, but it is also a very exciting one. By hiring employees you are adding a whole new dimension to your business. This is your team. Do your best to recruit and hire the most qualified people for the jobs, play by the rules set forth by the various government agencies, and keep your paperwork in order. If you do all of this, the business game will not be as intimidating. Here are some strategies and tips to help build and maintain a sound and satisfied business team.

- The skills and attitudes of your future employees will help build your business' credibility and reputation and those of its products or services. Look hard and long for the right members of your business team; it can make a difference in whether you win or lose in the business game.

- Consider using leased, contracted, or temporary employees. You pay a single set cost for your personnel through a negotiated contract. This single charge per employee covers salary and benefits and eliminates the need for most personnel paperwork.

- Medical exams cannot be used as a screening device for hiring employees. Their use is a tricky area even after you have hired someone. If you want to include medical exams in your hiring process, contact your workers' compensation department, as well as a professional adviser on the rules outlined in the Americans with Disabilities Act (ADA).

- The better prepared employees are to assume job positions, the less likely they are to feel out of place and look for employment elsewhere. Orientation provides an employee with information on company benefits or what benefit choices the employee has.

- Many state occupational safety and health agencies offer free, confidential, on-site consultation services for employers who want to ensure they are in compliance with all state and federal OSHA laws. Call your state department of labor to see if your state offers this valuable, helpful service.

- The unemployment tax is one tax you can help reduce on your own. By not overhiring and causing excessive layoffs, by keeping detailed records of why an employee was fired, and by challenging unfounded unemployment claims brought against your business, you will most likely reduce your tax experience rating and save yourself some money.

- Many of the state employment agencies offer free employer handbooks that explain the unemployment taxing and benefit procedures for their respective states. It would be worth a phone call to get this handbook before you hire employees.

- By keeping detailed personnel records, you help prevent costly government fines and establish a strong foundation for a well-managed human resources department.

- A company policy manual is critical in establishing clear communications with your future employees. Make it a priority, before you start hiring, to have your thoughts, procedures, and policies down on paper. It will be time well spent.

Helpful Resources

A Company Policy & Personnel Workbook
The Oasis Press/PSI Research
Grants Pass, OR
(503) 479-9464
(800) 228-2275

A great how-to guide for developing your own company policy manual. This book is ready to help you be a better employer by communicating your policies and procedures in a comprehensive and clear manner. $29.95.

Circular E, Employer's Tax Guide
Internal Revenue Service (IRS)
Washington, DC
(800) 829-3676

An IRS publication that explains federal income tax withholding and Social Security tax requirements for employers. *Circular E* also contains up-to-date withholding tax tables so you can determine how much federal income tax and Social Security tax to withhold from employee paychecks.

CompControl
The Oasis Press/PSI Research
Grants Pass, OR
(503) 479-9464
(800) 228-2275

This book simplifies insurance language and clearly spells out the workers' compensation process so you can better understand how to reduce your costs and premiums. $19.95 for paperback or $39.95 for 3-ring binder.

Draw the Line: A Sexual Harassment-Free Workplace
The Oasis Press/PSI Research
Grants Pass, OR
(503) 479-9464
(800) 228-2275

This business guide is designed to help you understand what constitutes sexual harassment and how to create a harassment-free workplace. The book features easy-to-follow steps for reducing sexual harassment, a sample sexual harassment policy, and what to do when a sexual harassment claim is filed. $17.95.

EEOC Technical Assistance Guide
Equal Employment Opportunity Commission
Washington, DC
(202) 663-4900
(800) 669-4000

A free listing of nonprofit resources offering technical assistance related to EEOC regulations. The EEOC is also a good place to find more information about the Americans with Disabilities Act.

Employer's Handbook
U.S. Immigration and Naturalization Service (INS)
Washington, DC
(800) 755-0777

A free publication to help employers deal with the department's procedures and forms. Call the number above or check your local phone listing for the INS office nearest you.

How to Comply with Federal Employee Laws
London Publishing
Washington, DC
(202) 296-7340

Updated in 1991, this easy-to-read book gives you the specifics you need to comply with federal employee laws. Good reference for the beginning business owner. Paperback edition costs $21.95 and includes shipping and handling.

The National Staff Leasing Association
Arlington, VA
(703) 524-3636

This association of leasing companies can provide information about the industry. It also helps establish standards and guidelines among its members.

People Investment
The Oasis Press/PSI Research
Grants Pass, OR
(503) 479-9464
(800) 228-2275

This book provides you with the step-by-step information for hiring the right people for your business. Learn about hiring practices, avoid legal problems, and start a personnel program the easy way! A great guide to completing many of the staffing activities described in this chapter. $19.95 for paperback or $39.95 for 3-ring binder.

Personnel Planning Guide
Dearborn Financial Publishing

Chicago, IL

(800) 621-9621

A handy reference for planning personnel needs. Worksheets and easy-to-read text help detail personnel records and procedures. Updated in 1990, the book costs $19.95.

Recordkeeping Requirements for Occupational Injuries and Illnesses
U.S. Department of Labor – OSHA

Washington, DC

(202) 219-6666

A free publication that details the recordkeeping requirements of federal OSHA. Call the number above or refer to your local phone directory under "U.S. Government – Department of Labor" for the regional OSHA office nearest you.

Safety Law Compliance Manual for California Businesses
The Oasis Press/PSI Research

Grants Pass, OR

(503) 479-9464

(800) 228-2275

Every California employer must now have an Injury and Illness Prevention Program that meets the specific requirements of Senate Bill 198. Already, thousands of citations have been issued to companies who did not comply with all seven components of the complicated law. Avoid fines by using this guide to set up a program that will meet Cal/OSHA standards. Includes forms. $24.95.

Social Security Administration

Washington, DC

(800) 772-1213

This toll-free number is available if you have any questions regarding Social Security.

Starting and Operating a Business in ... series
The Oasis Press/PSI Research

Grants Pass, OR

(503) 479-9464

(800) 228-2275

This helpful series of books covers all 50 states, plus the District of Columbia. Updated annually, each book contains the latest state-specific and federal business information available. Learn about your state's taxes, laws, and the agencies created to help you start and operate your business more successfully! A great resource for employer requirements! $24.95 for paperback or $29.95 for 3-ring binder.

Plan of Action — for Employees

Your company will need employees in the following areas:
☐ Full-time   ☐ Part-time   ☐ Temporary   ☐ Independent contractors

Use this planning tool to organize and prioritize the activities in this chapter that you need to do to start your business. Don't feel you have to list all the activities you have checked off. You can simply start with the top ten most important ones and go from there, or do whatever is easiest for you. Be sure to make plenty of copies of this cut-out worksheet for your planning and organizing activities for this chapter.

Action to be Taken	Begin Date	Who	Deadline

Plan of Action (continued)

Action to be Taken	Begin Date	Who	Deadline

Chapter 5

Producing Your Product or Service

Introduction

One of the most vital and dynamic aspects of your business will be the process of producing your product or service. To say nothing in business happens without a sale is obvious; however, it is the whole group of activities that takes place after the sale that can make your business unlike any other. How a business produces, packages, ships, and handles its goods, or how it ensures the performance of its service, is often unique and depends entirely on the particular product or service, be it a home-based catering business or a full-scale manufacturer.

Regardless of your type of business, planning for efficient production, warehousing, shipping and receiving, and inventory control is another important activity to think about before starting your business. Not only will knowing more about your production process and controls save you money, the planning will probably improve your productivity and streamline your operations.

This chapter has three main sections that cover some general aspects of production, warehousing and shipping, and inventory monitoring. The main goal of each of these sections is to prompt you into knowing more about these vital areas of your business. This post-sale aspect of your business is closely related to your financial management side as well.

It is the numbers and systems of these areas that will help you determine cost-of-goods, prices for your products or services, and how much inventory is needed for normal production. In each of the following sections, pay particular attention to the planning questions. They will be valuable strategies for you to think about when playing the business game.

First Aid for Producing Your Product or Service

 Many of today's general business books cover some aspects of production, warehousing, shipping, and inventory, including the *Starting and Operating a Business in . . .* series from The Oasis Press. However, if you are looking for additional, in-depth resources on these subjects, some first-aid resources to check into would include *Fundamentals of Inventory Management and Control* and *How to Plan and Manage Warehouse Operations*, which are both available through the American Management Association (AMA).

Fundamentals of Inventory Management and Control
How to Plan and Manage Warehouse Operations
American Management Association (AMA)
New York, NY
(518) 891-5510
(800) 225-3215

For more detailed descriptions of the above titles and additional books and sources of information regarding production and warehousing, see the Helpful Resources section at the end of this chapter, or research the business section of your local library.

Production

Production is the heart of every business. The reason people get into business is to produce a product or service. As a result, you should spend a great deal of time determining how you will produce what you are in business to sell, whether it includes manufacturing a product or delivering a service.

At first, your production will probably be small in relation to what you hope your future production will be. So to begin with, try to determine your start-up production needs as thoroughly as possible. By determining your production needs and their costs, you will have a better basis on which to figure the prices you will ask for your product or service.

You need to budget time for determining your product's or service's price. You may even want to consider test marketing your product or service before bringing it out to full-scale production. This means bringing your product or service to your market on a small-scale basis to test its attributes and salability.

You can test market different prices to see which one sells the most; you can test market different packaging methods to see which one receives the best response; or, you can test market different product features or service methods to see which is the most attractive to your target market. Refer to The Oasis Press book, *Power Marketing for Small Business*, for more on test marketing.

No matter what you decide to do to help determine your product's price, packaging, and shipping or your service's price and procedures, you will be ahead of the game if you take the time to evaluate your production process, needs, and costs. The checklists in this section should inspire you to look at this aspect of your business and be as thorough as possible in your figuring of production costs and setting of production goals.

Determining Your Unit Cost Checklist

Use this checklist to help determine your overall production needs and costs and your cost per product produced or service rendered (unit cost). If needed, find the services of a business consultant with expertise in production to see if you are on the right track. Finding out this information now will only encourage success in the future.

- ☐ Establish a list of the production equipment and machinery you will need to start production of your product or service.

  - ☐ Indicate how much each piece of equipment or machinery will cost you for initial start up and for monthly ongoing use.

☐ List what raw materials you will need to produce your product or service. Be sure to include every item involved in your production process.

    ☐ Indicate how much each piece of raw material will cost you for initial start up and for monthly ongoing use.

_____

_____

_____

_____

_____

☐ List any other one-time, start-up production costs you can think of that will influence your initial start-up expenses.

_____

_____

_____

_____

_____

☐ Then list all the ongoing production costs you can think of that will need to be budgeted for on a monthly basis, including those you listed for production equipment and raw materials. Consider some of the following for your list of ongoing production costs:

    ☐ Figure how many employee hours it will take to produce your product or render your service from start to finish. Be sure to factor their wages and benefits into the ongoing cost.

    ☐ Determine if your product is subject to efficiencies and improvements through machines or better production techniques. If so, what will the ongoing costs be to satisfy this need?

    ☐ Calculate the cost needed to run your company's machinery and equipment, such as power costs, employee wages, maintenance needs, and repair services.

    ☐ Include any ongoing shipping costs and packaging needs.

    ☐ If you will make service calls in a truck, include your auto expenses on the list.

☐ Include other expenditures, such as rent, taxes, accounting, personnel, and other costs needed to produce the product. (These costs generally cannot be applied directly to a unit, but they must be factored into the cost or you may not be able to make a profit.)

☐ Estimate the number of products to be produced or services to be rendered in a sample, normal production run for one month.

☐ Determine what it will cost you to produce one product or make one typical service call (a unit cost) by dividing your estimated, average number of products produced or services rendered for one month by the overall estimated ongoing production costs for one month.

☐ Establish a price for your product or service once you know your unit cost.

☐ Estimate your costs for damaged, unacceptable, returned, or unsaleable goods.

Other Production Factors Checklist

Besides knowing your start-up and ongoing production needs and your unit cost, think about some other issues regarding your production process. From issues such as employee safety to shipping and receiving needs, this checklist provides you with some tips on what to think about when evaluating your production process.

☐ Evaluate if you will be able to produce or provide the quantity of products or services that could be potentially demanded. Think of several different demand levels to see if you can produce the necessary numbers.

 What are the impediments to producing more?

Is increasing production important to the success of the business?

Will you be able to maintain the growth? If not, what are the consequences?

☐ Investigate how the businesses and vendors you will be dealing with in your production process set up and handle the following issues:

☐ Credit policies;

☐ Delivery periods and schedules;

☐ Discounts;

☐ Invoice payment policies;

☐ Returns of damaged or defective products;

☐ Returns of unused products;

☐ Returns of unused supplies, materials, or products; and

☐ Shipping charges.

☐ Determine if your product will need a bar code. If so:

    ☐ Determine how to reproduce bar codes for your items.

    ☐ Get information about placement, registration, and industry specifications on bar codes from the Uniform Code Council, Inc.

☐ Check with local, state, and federal agencies to see if you will need any approval for selling or producing your product or service.

☐ A testing laboratory, such as Underwriter Laboratories (UL), must certify the safety or quality of your product before you can sell through some channels of distribution.

☐ Determine if you have guarantees from your vendors and suppliers of an acceptable supply of, and set prices on, the inventory items or raw materials needed for production. If not:

Are there alternative sources?

Can you increase your prices without seriously cutting demand?

What can you do to assure your quality meets and remains at a level demanded by your customers?

What can you do to assure yourself the quality of materials or products you purchase from other vendors remains at the level you expect?

☐ If you expand production, consider the changes that will be required.

    ☐ Additional people

    ☐ Additional equipment

    ☐ Additional space

    ☐ Additional money for inventory or raw materials

☐ Check into the cost of waste disposal as a result of production.

Will your production generate waste that is toxic or must be disposed of in a controlled way?

Are there any environmental laws you need to be aware of when planning your production process? See Chapter 6 for more information.

Can you recycle any by-products from your manufacturing or production processes?

☐ Be sure to develop an employee safety awareness program for the procedures and operations in the warehouse.

Will your production require special lighting, venting, or other accommodations to reduce the possibility of industrial accidents or illnesses?

Does your equipment and machinery have all the guards and safety devices they were designed to have?

Do you plan to have a safety training program for truck drivers, forklift operators, and other operators of equipment or machinery?

Do you have on file and available to all users Material Safety Data Sheets regarding each hazardous substance you are using in your operation?

☐ Think about how and where you should incorporate quality control into your production process.

Warehousing and Shipping

To produce a product, you will need warehousing — you may have a place of your own to warehouse your items, or you may have some other company warehouse them for you. In either case, you must provide a space for your raw materials or inventory items so they are readily available for production and shipping. Finding a suitable warehouse that will be convenient for you, your future employees, and your future suppliers and shippers is an important step for your production operation to run smoothly and come full circle.

In addition, if you start a mail order business, a manufacturing business, or any other business that requires you to ship to your customers, you will need to know about the many shipping alternatives and decide which one is best for your business. Besides the popular UPS and Federal Express options, you can ship by rail, air, and water. Keep in mind, in many cases, you can negotiate rates with these shippers. Find out how to qualify for special rates and learn the many different ways to reduce costs in this complex area of business.

Any new businesses will require varying degrees of warehousing and shipping capabilities. Whatever the facilities you are planning, consider the activities listed in this section's checklists. These checklists will get you thinking about and planning for this very strategic aspect of your production or performance.

Warehousing Planning Checklist

Knowing where to locate your warehouse and how it will be set up and maintained are critical steps for ensuring a smooth order fulfillment operation. Take the time to evaluate your warehousing needs and develop a plan of action.

☐ Determine where you will warehouse your finished products and the raw materials necessary for production.

 Will the warehouse be near or adjoining your business office, or will you need to rent warehouse space away from your principal place of doing business?

☐ Evaluate your warehouse location carefully. Check to see if the warehouse building has the following items or features:

☐ Easily accessible doors and access for all sizes of trucks that will ship your products or deliver your raw materials;

☐ Sufficient electrical wiring for both your present and future needs;

☐ Good locations for any signs identifying your company or providing instructions;

☐ Enough space for your start-up and future needs; and

☐ Adequate fire protection.

☐ Consider how you will lay out the warehouse so it is efficient and safe for everyone.

 What types of shelving and storage units will work best in the warehouse?

How will heavy pallets or packages be handled and stored?

How will supplies and inventory items be organized?

☐ Develop the required procedures between your sales or order entry department and the warehouse personnel to ensure accurate order fulfillment.

 What actions will cause an item to be shipped, delivered, or received?

Who will be responsible for initiating each action?

How will a purchase order flow through your operations?

What is the time frame from taking the order to shipping it?

☐ Develop a record of receiving and shipping for your warehouse operations.

☐ Check to see if there are any zoning restrictions regarding your type of business, product, or activity.

☐ If your products are environmentally sensitive or a fire hazard, consider the extra precautions you will need to implement in your warehousing operations.

Will you be covered by insurance in case of an accident?

What actions can you take to reduce the possibilities of an accident that would harm the environment?

What type of protective area must you have?

How will you dispose of all waste materials used in production or manufacturing?

How will you dispose of warehouse and office waste materials?

Shipment Planning Checklist

In most companies, the warehouse is where most shipping and receiving takes place because that is where the inventory, as well as the raw materials needed for production, are kept. Ensuring your shipping and receiving procedure runs smoothly is not only crucial from a production standpoint, it is just as important in terms of customer satisfaction and for building your business' reputation as a reliable source of product or service. Your dependability and promptness in delivering the product or service will go a long way in gaining your customers' satisfaction, referrals, and continued business.

Take the time to review what steps you will need to do to get your shipping and receiving department in shipshape.

☐ Determine how you will ship your product or deliver a service.

☐ Airplane   ☐ Owned truck

☐ Common carrier   ☐ Ship

☐ Leased truck   ☐ Train

☐ Investigate the transportation companies available in your selected means of shipping.

☐ Compare rates and services of all the available shipping companies and determine whether it is more of an advantage to use one company over another.

☐ Try to negotiate special shipping rates for incoming raw materials or outgoing finished goods.

☐ Choose the person who will be responsible for doing your shipping and receiving.

Will that person need special training in how to package your product?

What type of skills are necessary for shipping and receiving tasks?

☐ Find out how your shipments or containers need to be labeled.

Will they need to be specially marked?

What size specifications will you require for your packaging and boxing needs?

If shipping hazardous substances, fragile equipment, or food, what shipping labels or shipping standards must you use or follow?

☐ List what material-handling equipment you will need for packaging, as well as unloading and loading shipments. For example:

☐ Forklifts   ☐ Racks

☐ Handcarts   ☐ Shrink-wrap equipment and film

☐ Pallets   ☐ Wire cutters

_____

_____

_____

_____

☐ List what shipping supplies and equipment you will need for start up.

☐ Boxes

☐ Computer/bar code equipment

☐ Postage meter

☐ Scales

☐ Shipping labels

☐ Tape guns, staplers, sealers

_____

_____

_____

_____

☐ Consider developing your own shipping and receiving system by using your own trucks, if feasible.

 What are the advantages and disadvantages of doing this compared to using a common carrier?

How will you schedule your production?

Inventory Control

Most businesses have an inventory of items that are needed for production, as well as an inventory of finished products ready for shipment. Even service businesses often have an inventory of supplies that help them perform their services. Regardless, you are going to want to know how much stock you have on hand, when to reorder supplies, and how much finished product you have available. Consequently, developing an inventory system that will answer these and other crucial questions is a sound business practice.

Inventory control, in conjunction with accounting, will help you get a clearer understanding of the cost of doing business and let you know where your products and supplies are going. For some advice on developing your inventory control system, talk to existing business owners in a line of business similar to yours.

The checklist featured in this section is a brief rundown of some of the things to consider when thinking about how to run your inventory control system.

Inventory Planning Checklist

Keeping tabs on how materials are coming and going from your business is one way to streamline production, but knowing this information takes time and organization. A computer is extremely helpful for completing this activity, and you should really consider purchasing a good inventory program that will meet the needs of your business.

☐ Decide how you will keep track of your inventory.

    ☐ Computer program

    ☐ Inventory cards

☐ Determine how you will monitor the shipping and receiving of finished goods and raw materials.

☐ If you will have a computer system, consider some of the following questions to see if they apply to your situation and if your computer system will be able to include some of this information.

Will the inventory tracking system provide the accounting information you need?

Can the system track completed products as well as raw materials?

Will it be easy to take an inventory with the system?

Will you be able to relate reductions in inventory to specific sales, jobs, or products?

Will the system separate purchased items from produced items?

Will the system track work in progress?

☐ Decide which inventory system to use for accounting your inventory costs.

   ☐ Last in, first out (LIFO)

   ☐ First in, first out (FIFO)

   ☐ Average weighted cost

   ☐ Standard cost

☐ Determine when you will do a physical inventory.

Will you have periodic cycle counts?

Who will be responsible for doing these physical counts?

☐ Develop a reordering procedure for your business.

☐ Develop a system to alert you when to reorder.

☐ Develop a process to identify the most economical order quantities.

☐ Factor in lead-time for your reorder needs.

☐ Develop an identification system for your inventory items.

Is it easily understood?

Will you be able to put it into a computer program now or in the future?

Will it fit the needs of the business as it grows or changes?

☐ Determine if you will need to keep track of serial-numbered items. If so, how will you do so?

Strategies and Tips:

 Playing the business game demands you put a lot of time into planning — planning everything from what media to advertise on to how much start-up inventory your business needs. All this planning will require your time and energy and probably the advice from business consultants or how-to business books. Obviously, production plays a big part in your business' success and in satisfying your customers, so be sure to allow plenty of time for its planning. Be sure to review all the tips and advice you get and use the Plan of Action for Producing Your Product or Service worksheet on page 117 to organize and prioritize your thoughts.

- If you have a warehouse, you probably will have employees. Be sure to develop a safety program for the procedures and operations in the warehouse. To obtain help for developing a safety program for your area, contact your workers' compensation insurer or your state's occupational safety and health agency.

- Constantly seek lower shipping rates and special billing arrangements. Quite frequently, trucking companies have heavy loads going in one direction, but they return unloaded. When this happens, they will often give discounts on such routes.

- Consider having another company do your warehousing and shipping before you commit to leases, equipment, and inventory purchases.

- When you price a product, you probably will need to have a mark up from actual cost to retail of at least five times the cost. Therefore, if you price a product based on a production run of 100 when your competitor bases it on 1,000, your unit price will be much higher, and you will overprice your product. Conversely, if you think you can price a product based on a higher production run, you may not be able to produce the product in the larger quantities and will find there is no profit because of higher costs related to the small runs that you can afford.

Helpful Resources

Fundamentals of Inventory Management and Control
American Management Association (AMA)
New York, NY
(518) 891-5510
(800) 225-3215

Fundamentals of Inventory Management and Control (continued)

This practical, self-study course book gives you a thorough understanding of how inventory impacts the financial well-being of your company — as well as the hands-on techniques you need to effectively manage inventory. $130. A discount is available to AMA members.

How to Plan and Manage Warehouse Operations
American Management Association (AMA)
New York, NY
(518) 891-5510
(800) 225-3215

This comprehensive course book covers all the elements you need to develop a sound management program for your warehouse. This course book introduces you to the kind of planning that maximizes the effective use of space, equipment, and labor. It will help you improve your bottom line. $130. A discount is available to AMA members.

Inventory Management
U.S. Small Business Administration
Washington, DC
(202) 205-6665
(800) 827-5722

This booklet discusses the purpose of inventory management, types of inventories, recordkeeping, and the role of forecasting. $0.50 (50 cents)

National Association of Manufacturers (NAM)
Washington, DC
(202) 637-3000
(800) 736-6627 (Membership information)

The National Association of Manufacturers is the voice for manufacturing in Washington, D.C., promoting a policy agenda that will increase the competitiveness of American industry. It also publishes a variety of booklets and publications that are very useful for the beginning or existing manufacturer. Call the above number for more on the NAM publications list, or call the toll-free number for information on joining this organization.

Operations Management in Manufacturing
American Management Association (AMA)
New York, NY
(518) 891-5510
(800) 225-3215

This self-study course book helps to identify the major stumbling blocks confronting operations management and presents a practical framework for overcoming them. The book discusses several critical areas for manufacturing excellence, including the different types of inventory systems available, how to maximize the value added to products, and ways you can integrate Design for Manufacturing (DFMA) principles. $130. A discount is available to AMA members.

Uniform Code Council, Inc.
Dayton, OH
(513) 435-3870

To find out more about product bar codes, call the number above for advice and information.

Plan of Action for Producing Your Product or Service

Your company will be producing a:
☐ Product   ☐ Service

Use this planning tool to organize and prioritize the activities in this chapter that you need to do to start your business. Don't feel you have to list all the activities you have checked off. You can simply start with the top ten most important ones and go from there, or do whatever is easiest for you. Be sure to make plenty of copies of this cut-out worksheet for your planning and organizing activities for this chapter.

Action to be Taken	Begin Date	Who	Deadline

Plan of Action (continued)

Action to be Taken	Begin Date	Who	Deadline

Chapter 6

Environmental Options and Laws

Introduction

The recent tide of environmental opinions and concerns has changed the way many businesses function. Regardless of what you may think about the earth's environmental health, public opinion — and even state and federal laws and pending legislation — will most likely dictate how you operate your business so it is more environment-friendly.

As a result of the recent environmental movement, the U.S. government has passed more than a dozen environmental laws. The most prominent of these laws are:

- The Comprehensive Environmental Response, Compensation and Liability Act (CERCLA), or more commonly known as the Superfund law;
- The Hazardous Materials Transportation Act (HMTA);
- The National Environmental Protection Act (NEPA); and
- The Resource Conservation and Recovery Act (RCRA).

The other laws cover safety and health; water, air, and noise pollution; and wildlife. In addition to these, most states have their own set of environmental laws. It will be your responsibility as a new business owner to find out which local, state, and federal environmental laws pertain to your particular product or service. Remember that environmental law is a dynamic area — what is merely an option today may be a law tomorrow.

With this thought in mind, this chapter provides tips for you to start developing a cost-effective environmental plan for your new business, in addition to helping you be aware of some of the current environmental requirements that apply to all businesses. The chapter takes you through the five R's of managing your business materials to dealing with hazardous materials legally and safely. The chapter concludes with a section on how to increase your energy and resource efficiency.

First Aid for Environmental Concerns

 *The Business Environmental Handbook* by Martin D. Westerman is a comprehensive book that leads you step-by-step through the process of developing an environmental plan to make your business more efficient. This book shows you how to be environment-friendly. Much of the information in this chapter is drawn from *The Business Environmental Handbook*. You may purchase this book from any local bookstore or order directly from the publisher.

The Business Environmental Handbook
The Oasis Press/PSI Research
Grants Pass, OR
(503) 479-9464
(800) 228-2275

Getting Started

Many opportunities to make your business environment-friendly are available in today's pro-environment atmosphere. However, don't try to do all the activities mentioned in this chapter at once. Developing an environmental plan is most likely an optional activity for you at this point in time, and simply taking the time to learn more about it is a step in the right direction. Start with the checklist activities that are the easiest and most convenient for you to implement, and go from there.

By thinking about ways to conserve and recycle now, you can be better prepared for any future legislation that may affect how you run your business. In addition to being better prepared, it really does pay to conserve and recycle. Your business can cut costs on energy bills and office supplies, plus you can earn money by producing extra energy or selling recyclable items.

A big part of any environmental plan is how well you manage the materials you will use for producing your product or performing your service, plus the materials you will use in everyday business operations, such as paper, gas, and electricity. Effectively managing your materials can reduce your waste and disposal costs by at least 30 percent. To successfully manage your materials and to begin formulating your own environmental plan, incorporate the five environmental R's into your business practices. The five R's are rethink, reduce, reuse, recycle, and results. The fifth R is achieved by carrying out the first four.

The five R's each have their own checklist of activities in this section. They follow the Getting Started Checklist listed below. Use these checklists to develop a cost-cutting, money-saving environmental plan for your new business.

Getting Started Checklist

The hardest part of any endeavor is getting started. As you begin thinking about an environmental plan for your new business, consider the strengths and limitations of your suppliers, locality, facility, and staff. All these factors will influence which actions you choose to carry out in your environmental plan. The checklist below will help you address the preliminary considerations for creating your plan.

☐ Create a company environmental mission statement, and include it as a policy in your company manual.

 Are you going to take an active part in helping the environment, such as sponsoring community clean-up or tree-planting projects?

Or, are you going to limit your environmental actions to simply ensuring that your company practices do not harm the environment?

☐ Demonstrate support for your environmental plan to your employees and suppliers. Options could include that you:

    ☐ Offer bonuses or other incentives to employees who suggest environment-friendly changes in company practices.

    ☐ Prepare a letter that states your preferences in packing materials and packaging, and send it to your suppliers.

☐ Encourage any future employees to look for wastes and suggest any improvements.

☐ Determine if your suppliers can provide you with recycled or environment-friendly materials.

☐ Research the recycling and composting options available in your area.

 Is there a recycling or composting program available? If so, what are the requirements to participate?

Are there any composting requirements for your state? Check with your state's environmental protection agency.

☐ Ask your utility company if it provides conservation kits. If so, get one.

☐ Determine the limitations of your facility, such as the amount of indoor and outdoor space available for recycling or composting.

☐ Consider writing a policy outlining your commitment to the environment and each employee's responsibility to uphold this commitment. Include the policy in your company policy manual.

☐ Start with low-cost/no-cost measures, such as providing ceramic mugs to employees rather than disposable cups for hot coffee or tea.

Rethink Checklist

By simply thinking through how your day-to-day activities will operate, you can discover many areas where you can make changes that will be environment-friendly and save you money. If you do an operations section for a business plan, this information would be very impressive to include, and any potential investor would note your extra effort. (See Chapter 7.) Also, if you are creating a business plan, but are only in the research stage, be sure to file your findings from the activities listed in this checklist in your business plan file for future reference. The activities below provide options for you to consider.

☐ Think about how your business will operate, and determine what will be thrown away and why.

    ☐ Eliminate, revalue, or reorient materials that will be thrown out.

☐ Make a diagram depicting the flow of materials from where they will enter your business to where they will exit. Make a separate diagram for each process and procedure.

    ☐ Determine if all the products and materials you anticipate using are really necessary to your business.

    ☐ Examine the possibility of consolidating or eliminating steps, based on the diagram.

☐ Purchase supplies with minimum packaging materials.

☐ Request your suppliers to use recyclable or biodegradable packaging wherever applicable.

☐ Research how your business can produce less waste for your customers once you are up and running.

 For example, if you are producing a product, are you using the least amount of packing materials possible?

Reduce Checklist

Source reduction — reducing the amount of materials you use for a particular project — is the key to reducing your waste output. Source reduction alone can cut your waste output by 10 to 30 percent. Some source reduction options are provided for you in the activities below.

☐ Purchase materials in bulk quantities whenever possible to eliminate excessive container and packaging waste.

☐ Make two-sided photocopies to reduce the amount of paper used.

☐ Remove your company name from unwanted mailing lists so your junk mail is reduced.

☐ Estimate equipment usage and rent or borrow, rather than buy, items you will rarely use.

☐ Plan to use biodegradable, recyclable, reusable, or no packing materials whenever possible.

Reuse Checklist

Reusing materials rather than buying new ones is an excellent way to help reduce waste, cut business expenses, and implement an environment-friendly activity.

The activities below will give you some ideas on where to start. This checklist is brief, but it gives you some clues as to what to look for. Be sure to evaluate your particular business for other opportunities to reuse materials.

☐ Furnish your office with pre-owned, quality equipment wherever possible.

☐ Use the blank side of used paper for messages and scratch pads.

☐ Reuse packing materials or return them to the supplier.

☐ Investigate starting a materials exchange program — both in-house and with other businesses in your location.

Can waste materials from one department be put to good use in another? For example, if one department generates paper as waste, bind it into scratch pads for other departments, such as accounting, to use.

Do you generate waste materials that another company can use? For example, your old wooden pallets can be useful to a company that produces mulch from wood.

☐ Reuse materials, such as file folders and inter-office envelopes, as often as possible.

☐ Recharge printer cartridges and re-ink printer ribbons.

Recycling and Composting Checklist

Recycling and composting are two methods you can use to reduce your waste disposal costs. In some areas, you can even earn a profit from recycling. Many states also encourage recycling efforts. Check with your local and state authorities to determine what, if any, of the following activities are optional or required for your business location. This checklist will get you to thinking about your recycling and composting efforts.

☐ Plan to purchase recycled-content materials to stimulate the recycling market.

☐ Decide what materials your business will recycle.

☐ Research your local recycling options.

What materials are recycled in your area?

Do recyclers require a minimum amount of materials?

Do recyclers charge to pick up materials?

Do recyclers pay for materials?

☐ Estimate the types and quantities of recyclable materials your business will generate.

☐ Calculate the potential savings or profits from recycling.

☐ Consider purchasing a compactor if you will generate 1,000 pounds or more of cardboard per week.

☐ Develop a recycling policy to include in your company policy manual.

☐ Provide adequate space for your recycling or composting operation. Consider:

How much material do you plan to recycle or compost per week?

What types of material will you recycle?

Does your state require landscape trimmings and other compostable materials to be separated out of regular garbage? (Nearly 30 states require that you do.)

How often will recyclable materials be picked up or delivered?

☐ Place recycling boxes near copy machines, fax machines, and computer printers, so it is convenient to put paper in them.

☐ Consider composting if your business will generate a pound or more of "wet" garbage per day and it is acceptable within your zoning guidelines. See the Glossary for a definition of wet garbage.

Hazardous Materials

A hazardous material is defined as any material or substance that is caustic, flammable, corrosive, reactive, or toxic. This covers a wide range of materials, including highly publicized toxins, banned pesticides, and even everyday household items, such as a can of Raid.

You are responsible for any hazardous material you use in your business and any damage it may cause. There is no statute of limitations on the damage caused by hazardous materials. For example, if you form a corporation that is later dissolved, under the Superfund law, officers and shareholders continue to be liable for any environmental damage caused by the corporation's hazardous materials.

This section provides two checklists to help you handle hazardous materials successfully and legally and reduce your liability.

The checklist activities that are required by law for all companies that handle hazardous materials are followed by an (R), which stands for "required." Some of the activities in the checklists are presented as options, yet may be required for some companies — the determining factor is how much hazardous waste your company will generate and how toxic the waste will be. Again, be sure to do your business game homework here. Find out what applies or does not apply to your business.

For more information on the legalities of handling hazardous materials, refer to *The Business Environmental Handbook,* the U.S. Environmental Protection Agency (EPA), and your state and local environmental departments.

Successfully Handling Hazardous Materials Checklist

Hazardous materials can cause harm to areas far outside the area of intended use. Not only can hazardous materials affect employee health, insurance costs, and real estate transactions, they can also increase your liability to the community at large. This checklist will help you set up procedures for successfully handling hazardous materials that are necessary for your business process.

☐ Create a written statement that clearly identifies your company's policies and objectives pertaining to handling hazardous materials and include the policies in your employee handbook.

☐ Plan to select a coordinator or committee to assess hazardous material inputs and outputs once your business is up and running.

☐ Set up a recordkeeping system and maintain a log of all actions and efforts pertaining to hazardous materials. (R)

☐ Determine which category of hazardous waste generator (listed below) your business will be considered. These definitions are set by federal law. For more information, contact your local solid waste management department or your regional office of the EPA.

   ☐ Household or conditionally exempt small quantity generator

   ☐ Moderate or medium quantity generator

   ☐ Large quantity generator

☐ Research the laws and reporting requirements for your level of hazardous waste generation.

   ☐ Compile a list of required permits and other environmental requirements from all local agencies.

☐ Contact your local solid waste management department and ask about disposal options, if you are a conditionally exempt small quantity generator. If you are a moderate and large quantity generators, you must comply with federal laws.

☐ Rethink how your business will operate and eliminate or reduce the amount of hazardous materials used, wherever possible.

☐ Obtain American LabelMark's Hazardous Materials Identification System (HMIS®) labels for all hazardous materials you will use. (This is one way to satisfy federal OSHA's hazardous communication standard requirements.)

☐ Investigate creating in-house programs and participating in out-of-house programs for reusing hazardous wastes, such as chemical compounds, solvents, lubricants, and coatings.

☐ Make arrangements to utilize local recycling programs for materials such as oil and antifreeze.

☐ Create an in-house means or hire a licensed contractor to detoxify or neutralize hazardous wastes. (R)

☐ Schedule a review of your business practices before you open your business.

  ☐ Look for areas where hazardous materials can be further reduced.

  ☐ Look for any areas or uses that could cause you to be held liable for damages.

Controlling Your Exposure to Liability Checklist

This checklist will help you reduce your exposure to liability for hazardous materials; however, the laws governing hazardous materials are constantly evolving, so you will need to stay aware of current legislative activity.

This checklist is in no way comprehensive. It is merely intended to make you aware of the types of requirements you will need to comply with once your business is up and running. Be sure to check with your local authorities, and with your regional office of the EPA, to find out exactly which laws apply to your company.

☐ Research discharging and reporting requirements for hazardous materials and be sure that you comply with every requirement. Do not take shortcuts or overlook even the smallest detail. (R)

 Be aware that if you discharge hazardous materials illegally and then file false reports, you may be prosecuted under the Racketeering Influenced and Corrupt Organizations (RICO) Act.

☐ Check the legality of selling or transferring hazardous materials before doing so. (R)

☐ Set up a check system to ensure that all hazardous substances have been properly treated before they are discharged. (R)

☐ Obtain the services of a licensed and bonded contractor to transport and dispose of your hazardous wastes. (R) (You may be able to obtain a license to do this yourself, but doing so will increase your liability.)

    ☐ Require proof that the contractor meets all legal requirements.

    ☐ Ask for references and check the reputation of the contractor.

☐ Post or centrally locate Material Safety Data Sheets (MSDSs) for all hazardous materials your business will handle. (R)

    ☐ Contact your local occupational safety and health office for more information on MSDSs.

    ☐ Train each employee who will handle hazardous materials about how to understand and use the information on the MSDSs.

Increase Your Energy and Resource Efficiency

This may come as a surprise to you, but utility companies are all too happy to help you increase your energy efficiency. It is cheaper for them to help you install efficient energy and water systems than it is for them to find and develop new sources of energy and water. Many offer free services and low- or no-cost loans to help you install energy- and water-efficient equipment. This section provides checklists for energy, water, and transportation efficiency measures. Consider implementing some of these optional measures into your environmental plan.

Energy Efficiency Checklist

You can "create" energy for your business by investing in efficient equipment and cutting waste. Every function of your business you improve, and every energy waste you eliminate, is money in your pocket.

☐ Make energy efficiency a company policy.

☐ Determine the most cost-effective sources of energy for your business.

    ☐ Compare the rates from different sources of energy in your area, such as solar power, hydro-electric power, natural gas, coal, or oil-fired power plants.

☐ Install window films, shades, or curtains on all windows to block the sun's heat during the hot season. This will help reduce the power needed for air conditioning.

☐ Ask your local utility companies what assistance programs they offer for making your business more energy efficient.

☐ Investigate using solar thermal units for space and water heating.

☐ Install water heater jackets where appropriate, and insulate hot water piping throughout your building(s).

☐ Preset heating and air conditioning thermostats, and turn water heater, refrigeration, and freezer thermostats to the minimums allowable for health codes and energy conservation.

☐ Use task lighting for work areas and stations — that is, place lamps on individual desks and over copy holders for computers rather than using overhead lights to light an entire room.

☐ Turn off or "standby" all lights and equipment when they are not in use.

☐ Use daylighting as much as possible. See the Glossary for a definition.

  ☐ Install interior lights that will automatically dim or shut off when bright daylight is available.

☐ Install only energy-efficient lighting fixtures.

☐ Install dimmers, occupancy sensors, timers, or trip switches to reduce energy usage.

☐ Investigate cogeneration. See the Glossary.

Water Efficiency Checklist

By using water efficiency measures, you can cut your business' water consumption by up to 25 percent a year. The activities below will help you use your water efficiently and save money.

☐ Make efficient water use a company policy.

☐ Review all activities and processes for water efficiency.

☐ Install low-flow or laminar flow aerators at all sink faucets.

☐ Install low-flow shower heads with on-off flow interrupters, if you are going to provide showers for your employees.

☐ Install ultra-low flush toilets.

☐ Xeriscape. In other words, landscape with drought-tolerant flora appropriate for your climate.

☐ Use positive shut-off nozzles on all hoses.

- [ ] Water the landscape only when needed.

  - [ ] Water only in the mornings and evenings, on overcast days, or when the area to be watered is in the shade.

- [ ] Check to see if you can use greywater for irrigation purposes.

- [ ] Use standing or drag-out rinses, extra tanks for cascade rinsing, or counter-current rinsing wherever appropriate for manufacturing processes.

Transportation Options Checklist

Everybody in business has to get to and from work, transport a product, or meet with customers. In fact, 26 percent of the country's energy resources, such as gas and oil, are consumed by the transportation sector each year. As you make plans to start your business, consider the cost-saving transportation options and alternatives presented in the activities below. They may provide you with some money-saving measures. These activities are optional and are simply provided for your review and consideration.

- [ ] Create a transportation utilization list to help you understand what your transportation needs will be.

  - [ ] List each vehicle or form of transportation you will use.

  - [ ] After each vehicle, write a description, considering the following:

    Where will you use your vehicles?
    What will they cost you?
    Are your intended vehicles the best to use for your tasks?
    Will your vehicles carry optimum loads?

- [ ] Minimize your vehicles' environmental impacts by performing proper maintenance procedures.

- [ ] Explore uses of alternative vehicle types and fuel or power sources for specific purposes in your business.

- [ ] Create an employee commute-trip-reduction program.

  - [ ] Provide free or discounted public transit passes to your employees to encourage public transit use.

  - [ ] Post public transit schedules.

  - [ ] Offer incentives to carpoolers, such as free parking or a cash bonus.

  - [ ] Provide a guaranteed ride home for carpoolers who have to work late or leave for domestic emergencies.

☐ Consider providing an on-site day care facility. Besides reducing gas consumption, it also is beneficial for reducing employee time off and turnover and promoting employee morale and productivity.

☐ Encourage employees who live nearby to ride their bicycles or walk to work.

   ☐ Provide showers and a safe place to store bicycles for employees who wish to bicycle to work.

☐ Consider telecommuting as an alternative for those employees whose position it applies to. This way, those employees would not have to physically commute to the office every day.

Strategies and Tips

As you have seen from the activities listed in this chapter, being environment-friendly can actually save you money and in some instances, increase your profits. Here are some additional tips for maintaining an environment-friendly business. A listing of resources you may find helpful is included after the tips.

- Stay informed about environmental issues pertaining to business in general.
- If you can generate excess electricity, your local utility company is required to purchase the excess from you.
- Create your own environmental business practices before you are required to do so by law. It will be much more cost-effective to stay ahead of environmental regulations than to play catch up.
- Avoid the use of hazardous materials as much as possible.
- Document all your environment-friendly actions for future use in a business plan or company promotion.
- Take advantage of green marketing opportunities. Refer to *The Business Environmental Handbook* for more information on green marketing.

Helpful Resources

A Guide to Resource Efficient Building Elements
Center for Resourceful Building Technology
Missoula, MT
(406) 549-7678

A Guide to Resource Efficient Building Elements (continued)
A handy guide for making your building more efficient. Call for ordering information. $25.

BioCycle
Emmaus, PA
(610) 967-4135

A monthly magazine on solid waste management with an emphasis on composting. Call for subscription information.

The Business Environmental Handbook
The Oasis Press/PSI Research
Grants Pass, OR
(503) 479-9464
(800) 228-2275

A comprehensive, step-by-step book that shows you how any business can be environment-friendly and environment-profitable. Provides a listing of helpful resources, EPA regional offices, and state environmental departments, as well as hazardous materials laws. $19.95.

Business Guide to Waste Reduction & Recycling
Xerox Documentation Subscription Service
El Segundo, CA
(800) 445-5554

A handy guide that offers information on waste reduction and recycling, especially for businesses. $25.

Hazardous Materials Identification System (HMIS)
American LabelMark/Labelmaster
5724 North Pulaski Road
Chicago, IL 60646-6797
(312) 478-0900

This company provides the colorful HMIS labels, which include a personal protection index. They also provide training materials. Write or call for more information.

National Lighting Bureau
Washington, DC
(202) 457-8437

Contact this organization for information on efficient lighting technologies.

National Recycling Coalition, Inc.
Washington, DC
(202) 625-6406
FAX (202) 625-6409

Contact this organization for free information on recycling.

Real Goods, Inc.
Ukiah, CA
(707) 468-9292

Real Goods is a catalog supplier of environment-friendly products and equipment. It also publishes the *Alternative Energy Sourcebook* and various books focusing on the environment and related issues. Call for ordering information.

Rocky Mountain Institute
Snowmass, CO
(303) 927-3128

This institute has researchers, publishers, and consultants who provide information on water and energy resources management.

Seventh Generation
Colchester, VT
(800) 456-1197

This company is a catalog supplier of environment-friendly products and equipment. Call to request a catalog.

Solid Waste Composting Council
Alexandria, VA
(703) 739-2401

Contact this organization for more information on composting solid wastes.

Solid Waste Information Clearinghouse
Silver Springs, MD
(800) 677-9424

Provides general information on solid waste. Also provides nationwide information referral.

Notes

Plan of Action for Environmental Options and Laws

Your company will:

☐ Develop a recycling program
☐ Get ideas on how to save on energy costs

☐ Review applicable laws
☐ Investigate environmental issues in your industry

Use this planning tool to organize and prioritize the activities in this chapter that you need to do to start your business. Don't feel you have to list all the activities you have checked off. You can simply start with the top ten most important ones and go from there, or do whatever is easiest for you. Be sure to make plenty of copies of this cut-out worksheet for your planning and organizing activities for this chapter.

Action to be Taken	Begin Date	Who	Deadline

Plan of Action (continued)

Action to be Taken	Begin Date	Who	Deadline

Chapter 7

Creating a Successful Business Plan

Introduction

What is a business plan, and why do you need to be concerned about writing one? This is a question many new business owners have, because until they open their own business and begin the process of looking for funding, some have never heard of such a document, much less know why and how they should put one together.

A business plan is an objective, written review of your business, which among other things, identifies areas of weaknesses and strengths, pinpoints needs, and helps you plan and achieve your business goals. In short, it gives you a clear idea of the obstacles that lie ahead and points out alternate game plans.

Most business plans are written for bankers, investors, or accountants and are used as a basis for a business to obtain start-up or necessary funding. But even if you don't need to find funding, going through the whole process of creating a business plan helps increase your chances of success. You will gain insight and knowledge about the markets and industries you will compete in, your finances, and your business' operations.

Don't be fooled: Developing a business plan is an organized process, and you will need to allow plenty of time for your research, organizing, and writing. This chapter is dedicated to helping you get a general overview of what you will need to do to write a successful business plan.

First Aid for Creating a Business Plan

Most of the information from this chapter comes from *The Successful Business Plan: Secrets & Strategies*, written by Rhonda Abrams. This book is a start-to-finish guide for writing a successful business plan. This comprehensive book takes you step-by-step from your initial concept to your completed business plan. The book includes tips on how to find funding sources, business plan secrets from heads of successful companies, and features the Abrams Method of Flow-Through Financials to help take the mystery out of financial reports and projections. The book is available in any local bookstore, or you can order the book directly from the publisher.

The Successful Business Plan: Secrets & Strategies
The Oasis Press/PSI Research
Grants Pass, OR
(503) 479-9464
(800) 228-2275

You will find this book of particular help if you are new to business, need help with your financial statements, or are looking for funding.

Your Business Concept

Before you can even begin to start the business plan process, you need to define your basic business concept — that is, you will need to explain in detail where and how you came up with your business idea or concept. Most entrepreneurs are inspired from various sources, such as previous work experience, education and training, personal interest and talent, or recognizing an unmet need in a particular area.

To ensure your business concept will succeed, you need to research it and determine if it is feasible; keep fine-tuning your concept as you obtain new information; and create a checklist to ensure your business concept and plan are compelling enough to hold the reader's interest. A well-developed business plan is critical for your company's success — don't take shortcuts!

The checklists in this section help give you an idea of the information necessary to accomplish all of these activities. More detailed explanations of these concepts are available in *The Successful Business Plan.*

Researching Your Business Concept Checklist

As Rhonda Abrams states in her book, "Don't try to be exhaustive in your research efforts; it's not necessary or possible." Your research efforts in the business plan process should revolve around basic questions about your business, yet be thorough enough to give yourself, and those reading your plan, confidence that the information you provide in the plan is accurate and based on reliable sources. The checklist below gives you some idea of the types of information you will need to research, as well as clues on where to obtain your research data.

☐ List what type of information you are likely to need to research your business concept.

Do you need to know the buying patterns of your target market?

How big does your market need to be in order to support your new business sufficiently?

What industry trends and standards apply to or affect your new business? Is your industry relatively healthy or is it experiencing some problems?

☐ Determine where you can go to get the information you need. Your options can include:

☐ Making a trip to your local library;

☐ Reviewing business and trade publications;

☐ Interviewing knowledgeable people in your market or industry;

☐ Talking to other businesses located near your proposed business location;

☐ Researching U.S. government resources and publications; and

☐ Calling your local and state governments for tips on where to look for various information on your type of business and appropriate industries.

Evaluating Your Business Concept Checklist

Whenever you do research, you are bound to come up with some new information that will affect how you view your original business concept. After you have completed your research, re-examine your basic business concept to see if your original concept needs to be modified or refocused. The business planning process is a learning process, and you should adapt your thinking to your increased knowledge. Being able to adapt is critical in any game, and the business game is no exception. Be prepared to reevaluate your business concept as new information arises. It will only prove your versatility and foresight as a business owner, and it will most likely keep you on the winning course.

Take the time to do the activities outlined in this checklist. With your research underway or finished, this checklist should be easier to complete. Regardless if you can do these activities at this point or not, do this evaluation at some point in the future.

☐ Determine if your product or service is viable. Consider:

 Can your product or service be developed in a reasonable period of time?

Are the costs of development reasonable?

Is there sufficient interest in the market for your product or service?

☐ Determine if your market is clearly identifiable.

☐ List your competitors.

_____

_____

_____

_____

_____

☐ Describe the economic health of your industry.

_____

_____

_____

_____

_____

☐ Explain any financial problems you anticipate.

_____

_____

_____

_____

_____

The Components of Your Business Plan

What to include in your business plan and how to arrange your information is a critical step to ensuring your plan gets read and improves your chances for receiving financing. The plan's information will convey the specifics of your business to potential investors, so you want it to be clearly written, well organized, and comprehensive.

Every business plan can vary in length and content, but for the most part, the components outlined and discussed in this section are a good rule of thumb for what to include in your plan. These components are:

- Executive summary
- Company description
- Industry analysis
- Target market
- Competition
- Marketing plan and sales strategy
- Operations
- Management and organization
- Long-term development and exit plan
- Financials
- Appendices

The executive summary is always the first section in your plan, but it must be written last. The rest of the sections may be worked on and arranged in any order; however, it is very important to arrange the sections in a manner that presents your business to the reader in the best possible way.

The checklists in this section are presented in the order that usually works best for most business plans.

Executive Summary Checklist

The executive summary is the most important section of your business plan because it alone persuades readers to take the time to find out more about your product or service, market, and techniques. If your executive summary is not compelling, it won't matter how innovative your business is.

The summary reflects the results of your planning and should be written after you have given careful consideration to all the other aspects of your business. Be positive, upbeat, and confident when writing the executive summary.

Remember, don't write the summary until you are done with researching, writing, and organizing the plan.

☐ Limit your summary to no more than two or three pages.

☐ Convey your sense of optimism about your business by using a positive, confident tone.

☐ Your summary must let the reader know that you have:

    ☐ A sound business concept;

    ☐ A thoroughly and carefully planned business venture;

    ☐ Capable management;

    ☐ A readily identifiable market;

    ☐ Significant competitive advantages;

    ☐ Realistic financial projections; and

    ☐ An excellent chance for investors to get their money back.

Company Description Checklist

Next, you must convey the basic details of your business to the reader before you discuss the more complex and intricate aspects, such as marketing, financial information, or new technology. The reader needs to know exactly what your company is all about, where it is located, and your legal form of business.

You also need to develop your mission statement and feature it in this part of your business plan. The company description section of your plan will probably take the least amount of time for you to prepare.

☐ State your company's mission statement.

☐ Indicate the legal form of your business, such as a sole proprietorship or a corporation.

☐ Provide the name of your chairperson, president, or chief executive officer.

☐ List other key management personnel, especially if they are known by the investor.

☐ Indicate how many people serve on your board of directors or advisory committee, if you have such a governing body.

☐ State the location for:

    ☐ Your company's headquarters;

    ☐ Your main place of doing business; and

    ☐ Any branches of your company.

☐ Describe the geographic area your company serves or will serve.

_____

_____

_____

_____

☐ State when your company was or will be founded.

☐ Describe your immediate development goals.

_____

_____

_____

_____

☐ Indicate which phase of development your company is in, for example, start up or mature.

☐ Briefly describe the financial status of your company.

_____

_____

_____

_____

Industry Analysis Checklist

No business exists solely by itself. Every business is part of a larger industry and is affected by the same factors that affect the industry as a whole. Analyzing your industry will increase your knowledge of what will contribute to your company's success. An industry analysis will also show the reader of your business plan that you are aware of and understand external business conditions.

The three areas you should focus on for the industry analysis section of your business plan are:

- A description of your industry;

- Current trends in your industry; and

- Strategic opportunities that exist in your industry.

☐ List the industries in which your company operates.

_____

_____

_____

_____

☐ Determine the size and growth rate of your industry.

☐ Research the effects of economic conditions and cycles on your industry and business.

☐ Describe how seasonal factors affect your industry.

_____

_____

_____

_____

☐ Describe how technological changes have affected your industry in the past five years.

_____

_____

_____

_____

Target Market Checklist

If you are using your business plan to obtain financing, a well-defined target market is critical. The checklist below is a general and brief overview of what to include in your description of your target market. A more detailed checklist regarding target market activities is listed in Chapter 3. Refer to that checklist for more specifics.

☐ Analyze and define your potential target market.

☐ Examine the buying patterns of your potential customers.

☐ Determine the buying sensitivities of your market.

☐ Assess the size and trends of your target market.

Competitive Analysis Checklist

Once you have a good idea who your target market is, you need to honestly evaluate your competition. This is an important part of your business plan, and one the reader will be interested in reviewing.

☐ Focus on identifying:

    ☐ Your major competitors;

    ☐ How you compare to your competition;

    ☐ Potential future competitors; and

    ☐ Barriers to entry for new competitors.

☐ Examine your competitive position in terms of customer preference and internal operational strengths.

Marketing Plan and Sales Strategy Checklist

Without a sound marketing and sales strategy, your business plan will be incomplete. In this section of your plan, you need to relate both of these aspects of your business and detail how each one will contribute to your overall business goals. The checklist below is a general one. Chapter 3 features a more complete discussion of marketing and sales strategies. Use both of these sources to help you develop a clear marketing and sales strategy for your new business.

☐ Define the message you want to send customers regarding your product or service.

_____

_____

_____

_____

☐ Describe the ways you can get that message to your target market.

_____

_____

_____

_____

☐ Identify the sales force and sales procedures you will use to carry out your marketing strategies.

Operations Checklist

Anybody reading your business plan is going to want to know how your business will operate on a day-to-day basis. Sometimes, taking your ideas and making them become a reality can be a challenging task. In this section of your plan, you need to describe to the reader just how you plan to or how you currently manage and run your business. This checklist gives you an indication of what to include in your operations section.

☐ Describe and evaluate the facilities in which your business will operate.

_____

_____

_____

_____

_____

_____

☐ Evaluate and assess your production plan.

  ☐ Include any information that shows how your process is efficient, such as how you recycle and reuse materials to cut costs. (See Chapter 6.)

☐ Examine how you organize your workforce in terms of producing or manufacturing a product or providing a service.

☐ Explain how you utilize new technology.

_____

_____

_____

_____

_____

☐ Describe how you fill orders and ensure delivery of your product or service.

_____

_____

_____

_____

_____

_____

Management and Organization Checklist

The success of a business is determined by the quality of its people. Investors often base their investment choices on the strength of the people involved in a business. Besides having a strong group of people, you also need a management structure and style that encourages people to work to their full potential.

When you develop this section of your plan, concentrate on the people who will be running your business and your management structure and style.

☐ Evaluate your management team. Include:

   ☐ Key employees/principals — limit yourself to discussing only five or six;

   ☐ Board of directors, if applicable;

   ☐ Advisory committee;

   ☐ Consultants and other specialists; and

   ☐ Key management personnel to be added.

☐ Determine what compensation and incentives you will offer your key employees.

 Will you offer a salary only, or will you offer bonuses, profit sharing, equity, or stock options?

☐ Obtain the services of an attorney and an accountant and indicate any other consultants or specialists you may need.

 Will you need management consultants, marketing consultants, designers, and industry specialists?

Long-Term Development and Exit Plan Checklist

Put yourself in the shoes of the investor for a moment. Before investing your money in any venture, wouldn't you want to know its long-term goals? Certainly! In addition, wouldn't you be interested in knowing how you are going to get your money back or exit from the venture? Again, you bet! This is the section of your plan where you answer these questions for your potential investors. Take the time to really evaluate where you want to be in say, five, six, or seven years. Be honest; discuss the problems and risks behind any of your goals and strategies. Review the checklist below to help you get going on this challenging evaluation of your business concept, operations, and overall goals.

☐ Determine your business' ultimate destination.

☐ Describe where you want your business to be in terms of your market in three or five years.

How many employees do you see in your business in the long term?

Do you want to be the largest business in your particular industry?

Do you have plans to open additional branches or locations of your business?

Will new facilities be a part of your future?

☐ Decide on a strategy that will take your business towards your long-term goals.

    ☐ Create a list of priorities.

    ☐ Assess the risks your business will face.

☐ Develop and clearly define your exit plan. See the Glossary for a definition.

Financials Checklist

As *The Successful Business Plan* states, "Numbers are neither magical, mysterious, nor menacing. They merely reflect other decisions you have made previously in your business planning." In short, every business decision you make is most likely associated with a number, and these numbers eventually make up your financials. In this section of your business plan, you need to ensure the numbers you provide are the result of careful planning. Don't be overwhelmed with the idea of preparing financials for your plan. If you don't feel confident enough to do it all on your own, then hire a financial adviser to help and teach you more about financials.

Use the checklist below to help you or your adviser, or both, get started.

☐ Indicate which type of accounting system is appropriate for your business:

    ☐ Accrual-basis accounting

    ☐ Cash-basis accounting

☐ When possible, use a spreadsheet program when preparing your financials.

☐ Provide financial projections for three to five years in the future.

☐ Present your financial projections honestly and conservatively.

☐ Use standard formats and financial terms.

☐ Prepare the following financial sheets and include them in your plan.

    ☐ Assumption sheet

    ☐ Cash-flow analysis

    ☐ Income statement

    ☐ Sources and uses of funds

☐ Follow the financial practices used in your industry.

Appendix Checklist

An appendix is used to reinforce the contents of your business plan. Only include an appendix to your plan if you feel it is necessary and the information is compelling. For example, you can provide specific details about market research, technology, location, and other aspects mentioned in your plan. New information should never be in an appendix of a business plan. Rather, all material in the appendix should be referred to in the body of your business plan. Here is a good overview of what to do regarding an appendix for your plan.

☐ Decide if you will need to include an appendix.

☐ Keep the appendix short — it should be no longer than the actual plan itself.

☐ Include the following items, as appropriate:

    ☐ Endorsements;

    ☐ Letters of intent or key contracts;

    ☐ Photos of your product, location, or other aspects of your business; and

    ☐ Technical information.

Using Your Plan

After you complete your business plan, put it to good use. Besides using your plan to obtain funding, use it as an internal planning tool. Periodically reviewing and evaluating your business plan will also help you reach the goals you set and stay competitive.

This section will explain how to make your plan presentable to others. When preparing your plan for distribution, consider how to prepare it so that it will have a maximum impact and be effective in helping you reach your objectives.

Preparing for Distribution Checklist

Before you begin distributing your plan, proofread your plan one last time and have someone else read it as well. When you are confident that your plan needs no further changes, complete the activities below.

☐ Create a cover sheet.

☐ Number the pages by section.

☐ Provide a table of contents if your plan is more than ten pages in length.

☐ Include a nondisclosure agreement — an example of this agreement is in *The Successful Business Plan* — and consult an attorney about your legal requirements.

Strategies and Tips

 A well-written, compelling business plan is essential for a business to receive funding; however, the process of developing a business plan takes time. It is not unusual for the process to take several months. While you don't want to rush the process at the price of sacrificing quality, there are some ways to make the process faster and easier.

- Get help. Start by using a comprehensive business planning guide, such as *The Successful Business Plan*, by Rhonda M. Abrams. This will answer most of your questions.

- Develop a research plan. If you outline all the information you are likely to need before you begin your research, you will avoid repetitious trips and tasks.

- Prioritize the most important sections of your plan. Allow plenty of time to work on those areas that are crucial to the success of your business.

- To be credible, your business plan will need to include all sides of your story — meaning always include the positive and negative aspects of any topic you are discussing.

- Organize your papers. In the process of developing a business plan, you will acquire a large amount of paper. Set up a filing system with individual files that correspond to each section of your plan. Begin filing material in the appropriate files immediately.

- Consult an accountant, lawyer, or management consultant.

- Since most business plans will be submitted to banks, it is important to know how a banker analyzes a business plan and what questions a banker asks during his analysis.

- Use a computer spreadsheet program, if possible, when preparing your business plan financials. If you have your own computer or if you have access to a computer and know how to use it, a computerized spreadsheet will make dealing with your financial materials much faster and easier.

- Don't be overwhelmed. If you stick to it, you can have a terrific business plan.

Helpful Resources

ABCs of Borrowing
U.S. Small Business Administration
Washington, DC
(800) 827-5722

This handy publication helps explain borrowing fundamentals in a concise, easy-to-read format. $1.

Current Industrial Reports (CIRs)
Economic Censuses
County Business Patterns
U.S. Bureau of the Census
Washington, DC
(301) 457-4608

CIRs provide information on production, shipping, inventories, consumption, and the number of firms manufacturing each product. The *Economic Censuses* report on monthly sales figures and trends for various industries, plus they provide information on sales by geographic area, zip code, and merchandise line. The *County Business Patterns* publication is useful in evaluating the performance and trends of your industry in your target location.

The Business Plan for Home-Based Businesses
U.S. Small Business Administration
Washington, DC
(800) 827-5722

If you are convinced that a profitable home business is attainable, this publication will provide a step-by-step guide to developing a business plan. $1.

DIALOG
(800) 3-DIALOG

Dialog, an on-line database, incorporates more than 300 different databases, including Dun & Bradstreet and Standard & Poor's. Dialog also contains Findex, which catalogs and describes industry and market research studies that are available commercially.

Financing Your Small Business
The Oasis Press/PSI Research
Grants Pass, OR
(503) 479-9464
(800) 228-2275

This step-by-step book shows business owners how to gain the benefits of debt while minimizing risks. Helps in evaluating company needs, identifying the best sources of funding, and preparing an effective financial proposal. A great help in learning financial information. $19.95.

Marketing Mastery: Your Seven Step Guide to Success
The Oasis Press/PSI Research
Grants Pass, OR
(503) 479-9464
(800) 228-2275

This book is very helpful for the beginning marketer looking for information on how to launch a new product, create an effective marketing strategy, and retain a core of satisfied-plus customers. $19.95.

The Money Connection
The Oasis Press/PSI Research
Grants Pass, OR
(503) 479-9464
(800) 228-2275

This book lists hundreds of sources of funding from SBA-approved banks to venture capitalists and Small Business Investment Companies. $24.95.

The New Product Development Planner
American Management Association (AMA)
New York, NY
(518) 891-5510
(800) 225-3215

This book guides you through every stage of the development process and takes you through every issue and consideration to increase your chances for success. $75.

Power Marketing for Small Business
The Oasis Press/PSI Research
(503) 479-9464
(800) 228-2275

A hands-on, easy-to-read book that details all aspects of marketing. Would be a great help in completing the marketing section of a business plan. $19.95 for paperback or $39.95 for 3-ring binder.

Raising Capital: How to Write a Financing Proposal
The Oasis Press/PSI Research
Grants Pass, OR
(503) 479-9464
(800) 228-2275

This book shows you how to write a financing proposal to secure business loans, venture capital, or grants. $19.95.

The Successful Business Plan: Secrets & Strategies
The Oasis Press/PSI Research
Grants Pass, OR
(503) 479-9464
(800) 228-2275

A start-to-finish guide to creating a successful business plan. Provides insider tips to writing a business plan and handy financials to make it easier to compile your information. Templates are provided for several of the worksheets found in the book. A standalone version is also available. $21.95 for paperback or consider the business plan kit for $49.95.

Venture Capital Primer
U.S. Small Business Administration
Washington, DC
(800) 827-5722

This publication highlights what venture capital resources are available, plus it explains how to develop a proposal for obtaining these funds. $0.50 (50 cents).

Notes

Plan of Action for a Business Plan

Your company will write a business plan: ☐ Yes ☐ No

Use this planning tool to organize and prioritize the activities in this chapter that you need to do to start your business. Don't feel you have to list all the activities you have checked off. You can simply start with the top ten most important ones and go from there, or do whatever is easiest for you. Be sure to make plenty of copies of this cut-out worksheet for your planning and organizing activities for this chapter.

Action to be Taken	Begin Date	Who	Deadline

Plan of Action (continued)

Action to be Taken	Begin Date	Who	Deadline
_____	_____	_____	_____
_____	_____	_____	_____
_____	_____	_____	_____
_____	_____	_____	_____
_____	_____	_____	_____
_____	_____	_____	_____
_____	_____	_____	_____
_____	_____	_____	_____
_____	_____	_____	_____
_____	_____	_____	_____
_____	_____	_____	_____
_____	_____	_____	_____
_____	_____	_____	_____
_____	_____	_____	_____
_____	_____	_____	_____
_____	_____	_____	_____
_____	_____	_____	_____
_____	_____	_____	_____
_____	_____	_____	_____
_____	_____	_____	_____
_____	_____	_____	_____
_____	_____	_____	_____
_____	_____	_____	_____
_____	_____	_____	_____
_____	_____	_____	_____
_____	_____	_____	_____
_____	_____	_____	_____

Buying a Business or Franchise

Introduction

Perhaps starting a business from the ground up isn't what you want to do, and you are more interested in the opportunities that lie with buying an existing business or franchise operation. If this is the case, this chapter will give you a general overview of what to do and what to investigate when purchasing an existing business or franchise.

Buying a business or franchise is an involved process and one that demands you retain the services of a qualified attorney and accountant. By reading this chapter, you will have a better idea of what to ask your advisers and what they should include in their investigations. As a general guide, try to keep these essential questions in mind when reviewing any business that is for sale:

- Can you earn a living from the business?
- Can you manage the business yourself?
- Can you enjoy the business?
- Can you afford to buy the business?

Be honest and candid in your answers to these questions, and if you answer "yes" to each of them, then you can proceed with your investigation of the potential business or franchise. Be sure you have covered all your bases! By buying a business the right way, you can jump out ahead in the business game, but by not doing it right, you could drop out of the game completely.

First Aid for Buying a Business or Franchise

 To avoid dropping out of the game completely, you can purchase a couple of book sources to help you stay on track. One such source is *The Secrets to Buying and Selling a Small Business* by Ira N. Nottonson. This handy book prepares a business buyer or seller for negotiations that will achieve win-win results when purchasing or selling a business.

Another book is *Franchise Bible: How to Buy a Franchise or Franchise Your Own Business,* written by Erwin Keup. This book is a comprehensive guide that explains in detail what the franchise system entails and the benefits it offers. The book contains an actual offering circular to familiarize you with the terms and considerations franchisees face. You can order these books directly from the publisher or purchase them from a local bookstore.

Franchise Bible
The Secrets to Buying and Selling a Small Business
The Oasis Press/PSI Research
Grants Pass, OR
(503) 479-9464
(800) 228-2275

Buying a Business

The idea of having an established customer base and receiving an income the first month after taking ownership of an existing business can make the decision to purchase an existing business over starting one from scratch very appealing. In fact, the cost of buying an existing business is usually comparable to the investment ultimately required in starting a new business. Indeed, many of the rigors and risks of starting from scratch are nonexistent with the successful purchase of an existing business; however, the purchasing process is not one to be taken lightly. For you to enjoy the advantages of owning an established business, you need to be well informed on how to:

- Properly research the business and the appropriate trade or industry;
- Consider the financial variables and growth potential of the business by examining the history and progress of its growth;
- Value the assets of the business and be careful to note potential obsolescence of inventory and equipment;

- Work with a potential partner or investor to ensure stability and control, being particularly careful to understand whether this person's goals and aspirations are consistent with your own; and

- Negotiate the sale to ensure you will get what you pay for and protect against misrepresentations.

In addition, you will also need to know about the closing of the sale and various tax and other legal considerations. To help you get an idea of what is involved in the purchasing process, the checklists in this section are designed to highlight important purchasing factors.

Before entering into negotiations with a seller, you need to commit yourself to the time and energy it will take to become familiar with purchasing terminology, procedures, and legal requirements. To help ensure your success in this particular aspect of the business game, gather a strong team of professionals, attend any related seminars in your area, and purchase helpful books on the subject, such as *The Secrets to Buying and Selling a Business* by Ira N. Nottonson. The majority of the checklists below are based on this very detailed and informative book.

Research Checklist

Before you even begin to do any prepurchase research, you need to seriously consider what type of business best fits your particular skills and talents. Know your strengths and weaknesses. Remember that nearly all businesses today need managers and owners with strong selling skills. In addition, understand your level of commitment to your future business and make sure your family is supportive and informed. With a review of these personal factors, you will then be better prepared to target specific businesses for research. Use this checklist for every business you consider purchasing.

☐ Develop your research questions so they are specific and direct.

Did the industry or trade grow in size last year?

How much is it expected to grow in the next year?

What products or services are in greatest demand? And by whom?

What problems do suppliers have providing products and a consistent price?

☐ Ask an existing competitor (or franchisee) for a general description of what the business and particular industry entails.

☐ Consult with your business consultant, attorney, and accountant to get their opinions on the business.

☐ Read trade magazines to inform yourself of the latest technology, trends, and innovations in the industry.

☐ Talk to the business' vendors and suppliers so you get a better view of the industry.

☐ Review the answers to your research questions and reevaluate them to glean even more information.

☐ Find out why the owner wants to sell the business.

Is any portion of the inventory or equipment becoming obsolete?

Does the owner know of a new competitor coming to the area?

Is the business unable to support the owner?

Is the owner simply wanting to retire?

☐ Consider your funding resources and the business' ability to service debt and provide you with an income.

Will you simply need to make enough to keep the business going and support your family?

Or, must the business help pay back the money you borrowed to buy the business?

☐ Examine and read the sales materials carefully.

☐ Do a historical analysis of the business.

☐ Get a feeling for the business' impact on its existing customer base.

☐ Talk with current customers, employees, and suppliers of the business to get feedback on the business and its product or service.

☐ Investigate whether there is a loyalty factor that will cause a degradation of the customer base after the sale.

☐ Visit the prospective business in person to get a first-hand feel and view of the facilities, the traffic patterns, the surrounding area, the population mix, and the neighborhood.

☐ Determine how the business' reputation will be affected if you take over the business.

☐ Ask yourself why you think you can make the business even better, if it is a profitable business. If it is an unprofitable business, ask yourself why and how you would do a better job.

Financial Considerations Checklist

The first decision you face as you consider buying a business is how to finance it. There are three essential factors involved in that decision: your cash return, your level of risk, and your financing method.

These three financial factors are briefly highlighted in the checklist below. Become familiar with these terms and make sure your accountant helps you evaluate them when considering any potential business purchase.

At this point, you need to be working with the seller in early negotiations to get access to the records and documents that will allow you to recognize the financial responsibilities of the business, both in the short term and the long term.

The success of negotiations depends in great part on the relationship established between the parties at the beginning of the buying and selling process. So if you can establish trust early on, you will find the process will go much smother.

- ☐ Compare the return your cash investment will yield in the existing business with the return it receives in its current stocks, mutual funds, or savings accounts.

- ☐ Obtain all previous tax returns, bank deposit records, and other financial records of the business to track its financial health and history.

  - ☐ Examine accounts receivables and collection policies.

  - ☐ Request the previous three years' profit and loss statements, balance sheets, and cash-flow analyses.

  - ☐ Review the business' financial history via the profit and loss statements and balance sheets.

- ☐ Recast the previous profit and loss statement to see what your profit would be if you bought the business.

- ☐ Thoroughly investigate the business' reputation and other intangible factors that might have an impact on its future.

- ☐ Determine the level of risk involved with the investment.

What are the financial percentages involved?

Is there any possibility that the equipment or inventory may become obsolete?

Does the business' success depend on the present owner's ability to sell, or is it because of her personal contact with key customers?

Is the location the most vital part of the business?

☐ Determine how you will finance your business purchase.

Will you have a cash-in-full purchase, or will you need a down payment and owner financing?

What funding resources do you need and possess?

What purchase alternatives are available, such as interest rate or length of purchase money promissory note, that might adjust the price and make the sale possible?

Valuing Assets Checklist

Once you have done as much general, prepurchase research as possible, and evaluated your financial considerations, you will want to look more specifically at your prospective business' selling price. An existing business offers many types of assets, and each asset's value will eventually be figured into the selling price in one way or another.

To determine the value of the asset variables, you will have to do some research on your own; consult appraisers, accountants, or attorneys; and request specific information from your seller. The checklist below is designed to help you value a business' assets so you can decide whether to proceed further into negotiations.

☐ Determine whether a business' equipment is outdated, obsolete, or state-of-the-art.

☐ If outdated or obsolete, calculate how much it will cost to update or replace the equipment to ensure the business' competitive edge and use this as a negotiating point for a lower price.

☐ Investigate whether the business' particular industry is expecting any technological innovations with equipment that may affect its operations.

☐ Check with the appropriate state or local authorities involved in maintaining ownership records and assure that there is not a lien or an encumbrance on the equipment.

☐ Review equipment maintenance records and status of company warranties.

☐ Personally evaluate the inventory of the business.

Is the inventory's volume currently too high or too low? Is it obsolete or valuable?

What dollar amount are you willing to pay for it as part of the purchase price?

☐ Make sure the seller actually owns the inventory, has paid for it, and has not pledged or otherwise used it for security.

☐ Ask if any real estate is involved with the purchase. If so, then have a separate analysis of the real estate done by a professional appraiser.

What is the fair market value of the real estate?

What is the value of the property without the business as a tenant?

Will the property be worth more as time goes on?

Is the property free and clear of all liens or encumbrances?

☐ Understand all the terms and conditions of the lease, if applicable.

☐ If a building is for sale, along with the business, determine if it is in good condition and have its value appraised.

Is asbestos present in the building?

Is there an environmental clean-up problem involved at the property?

Does it need a new roof?

What are the annual maintenance costs and repairs?

☐ Consider the value of the business' highly qualified employees and their relationships to the business' existing customer base.

☐ Evaluate the effectiveness and value of the business' location.

☐ Be prepared to pay for the benefit of a business that has a recognizable logo, an established trade name, or a favorable reputation.

☐ Determine the value of a business' computer hardware and software to make sure you are paying for an effective, efficient system.

☐ Determine if the absence or presence of competition for the business is desirable or not, and take that into consideration when assessing the selling price.

Investor or Partner Checklist

Some business sales can occur in one simple transaction with the buyer taking over the business right away and doing so on her own; however, many other business sales require the seller to stay on as a paid consultant, investor, or partner. Not all partners or investors are former owners, though such an arrangement is one way to creatively finance a sale. Often, buyers need the participation of other people for money, guidance, or actual labor. If you are considering taking on an investor or partner or becoming one yourself, the checklist below will alert you to some of the issues related to sharing control of your business. As always, consult an attorney and accountant before you finalize any investor or partnership deal.

☐ Be aware that by accepting investment capital, you are giving up a degree of control over your business.

☐ Know what your investor's or partner's goals are.

Are those goals consistent with your goals?

Will your business venture satisfy your investor's or partner's goals?

Do you think that short-term thinking by the investors to protect their investment might subvert your long-term goals?

☐ Consider a realistic timetable with the investor or partner for when the business will be able to pay back the investment, give a return on the investment, or buy out the partner, if that is your intent.

☐ Discuss the legal form of doing business, such as a partnership or corporation, with your partners or investors.

☐ Understand what joint and several liability is. See the Glossary.

☐ Determine if an employee or paid consultant can fill your need for expertise, rather than an investor or partner, should you only need a partner for his personal knowledge and experience in your type of business.

☐ Work out a comfortable buyout arrangement between you and your partners for when you choose to dissolve the partnership.

Negotiating Price Checklist

By the time you are ready to begin pricing negotiations, you have already had some initial contact with the seller. During this time, you have hopefully created an environment of trust and the seller realizes you are a serious, prospective buyer. The main factor that will affect the price negotiations will be how you pay for the business — cash-in-full or with a down payment and financing. You will need your accountant to help you with this part of the negotiations process. The checklist below gives you an idea of what to include in your price negotiations.

☐ Decide if you will do an all-cash deal or make a down payment with an owner-carry contract.

☐ If an all-cash deal, expect a bigger concession in the selling price.

☐ If a down payment deal, determine the amount of your initial down payment, negotiate the length of the note, and negotiate the interest rate.

☐ Once the down payment, length of note, and interest rate have been negotiated, you should be able to discuss a reasonable selling price.

☐ Remember the operating profit of the business is the key to creating a selling price, for example, a higher operating profit allows a seller to ask a higher price.

☐ Push for an allocation of the purchase price to specific assets in the sales agreement. Discuss the advantages of doing this with your accountant.

  ☐ Seek to maximize the amounts allocable to depreciable assets and any noncompetition covenant.

  ☐ Seek to minimize allocations to goodwill or land purchased.

☐ Look for hidden liabilities against the business and make sure they are taken care of in the sales agreement. For instance:

Are there any pending lawsuits?

Do any current employees have accrued vacation coming to them?

Do any employees have any close relationships with any large, existing customers?

Are there any unfunded pension plan liabilities?

What about any potential exposure to environmental clean-up costs?

Closing the Transaction Checklist

Once you have completed negotiations and are satisfied with the results, you will be ready to close the deal. To close a deal, you will need to do several activities, some of which are required legally. These requirements, as well as other activities, are listed in the checklist below.

☐ Retain an attorney to participate in drawing up the sales agreement.

☐ Comply with any bulk sale laws in your state by checking with the secretary of state's office for details. See definition for bulk sale laws in the Glossary.

☐ Be sure the acquired property is not subject to any recorded security interests or other liens beyond those disclosed by the seller. To do this, have your attorney conduct a thorough search of the appropriate offices.

☐ Have the seller obtain and furnish you with a certificate stating that sales and use taxes and unemployment taxes have been paid.

☐ Seek to hold back part of the purchase price as security to reimburse you for any misrepresentations as to assets or liabilities by the seller.

☐ Make provisions for acquiring customer mailing lists or any other collateral assets on which the continuity of the business may depend.

☐ Prepare *Form 8594* and file it with the IRS once the deal is closed.

☐ Check with your state government to ensure you complete any state requirements regarding the purchase of a business, such as bulk sales laws or notification of transfer of ownership.

Other Tax and Legal Considerations Checklist

Despite the activities listed above, there are some other items to consider when thinking about purchasing a business. This checklist attempts to compile a few of these miscellaneous, yet important items so you and your advisers don't forget them.

☐ Determine whether the sale of the business will result in a sales tax liability with respect to part or all of the purchase price.

☐ If buying a corporation that has not paid income taxes because of carryovers of net operating losses, be aware that you may be able to use only a small portion of those carryovers to shelter the income of the business once you become the owner.

☐ Check the seller's workers' compensation insurance rate to see how your rate will be assessed.

    ☐ Determine if you can succeed to the seller's rate or if you will receive a new one.

☐ Check the seller's experience tax rating for unemployment tax purposes, and if it is better than the tax rating you would receive as a new employer, then see if you can succeed to that favorable rating.

    ☐ Contact your state's employment service department for more information on succeeding to experience tax ratings.

☐ Understand your obligations under the Foreign Investment in Real Property Tax Act (FIRPTA) if you purchase real estate from a "foreign person."

    ☐ Contact the IRS for more information on FIRPTA.

☐ Hire a licensed expert to perform due-diligence environmental testing of the property. This is especially important if the business handles or produces hazardous wastes. The term, "due-diligence," is defined in the Glossary.

    ☐ Inspect the neighboring properties, if possible.

☐ Pay close attention to property boundaries. Even if the waste comes from a neighboring property, you will be liable for any waste found on your property.

☐ Negotiate with the owners of any adjoining empty lots to control and account for all dumping there.

☐ Ask the current owner if he has had any problems with sick building syndrome. See the Glossary.

☐ Determine if underground tanks are present on the property. If so, consider:

What were they used for?

What is the viable lifetime of the tanks?

Is there evidence of contamination or damage to the ground, groundwater, flora, or fauna?

Will you have to fill or remove the tanks?

☐ Consult your state environmental department to determine which requirements apply to the business you are buying.

☐ Determine if operating licenses or leases can be transferred or if you will need to apply for new ones.

☐ See if you will be able to transfer intangible property rights, such as patents, trademarks, or copyrights.

☐ Have your attorney review all provisions of key contracts, leases, or any other legal arrangements that have a significant effect on the business.

Buying a Franchise

Buying a franchise is different than buying an existing business because of the unique relationship that exists between the franchisor and franchisee. In a franchise relationship, you can enjoy less risk, more management support, more profits, additional financing, and numerous advertising benefits. On the other hand, you pay fees, royalties, and down payments, plus you don't have as much control or flexibility in running the business.

Regardless, franchising is a very common way to start a new business in today's business world, and if you are still considering ways to start your business, the information in this section may prove helpful. Review the checklist in this section and the Helpful Resources at the end of this chapter for more on how to investigate and buy a franchise. Keep in mind that the process of buying a franchise demands careful investigation and professional assistance from attorneys and accountants.

Buying a Franchise Checklist

The checklist below is a general overview of what to think about when considering buying a franchise. The book, *Franchise Bible*, has a more detailed discussion of the factors involved in franchising in its Part 1, Buying a Franchise.

If you are seriously considering a franchise as your new business, you may find this book very helpful. *Franchise Bible* has been recently revised to cover the Federal Trade Commission's newly mandated rules regarding franchise disclosure statements.

☐ List the franchises that interest you the most.

_____

_____

_____

_____

_____

_____

_____

☐ Research the names and addresses of these franchises. See Helpful Resources on page 170 for hints on where to look for franchise listings.

☐ Write to each of the franchise headquarters and request a copy of its uniform franchise offering circular.

  ☐ Investigate what an offering circular should contain. (In January 1995, the Federal Trade Commission's (FTC) newly revised mandatory rules regarding the circular's content went into effect.)

☐ Evaluate each franchise by reviewing its circular and by interviewing existing franchisees, failed franchisees, suppliers, and the franchisor.

☐ Make a final selection and move towards negotiating a contract.

☐ Hire an experienced franchise attorney, who is also familiar with the new FTC franchise law that became effective in January 1995, to review disclosure statements and help you with any negotiations.

☐ Review the contract and have a clear idea of what should be included in the document. Consider:

What are the initial costs and fees of the franchise?

Where will the location of the franchise be and will other franchisees be allowed in the same area?

Who controls hours and prices?

What kind of training will you receive as a franchisee?

How will any co-op advertising work?

What kind of financing is available through the franchisor?

What items must you purchase from the franchisor, and do you have the option to buy them locally, if they are cheaper?

☐ Investigate the use of the franchisor's trademarks and service marks.

Is the trademark well known?

What rights do you have as a franchisee for use of these marks?

Strategies and Tips

As a prospective buyer of an existing business or as a prospective franchisee, you need to gain as much information and knowledge as you can about the buying process, including negotiations and contract writing. As mentioned before, this can be a highly complicated process, so be sure to retain the services of an experienced attorney and review the tips and helpful resources mentioned below.

- Business brokers and realtors can be excellent sources for finding a business that is for sale. You can also look for ads in local newspapers, or ask your lawyer or accountant.

- An attorney and accountant are necessary members of your buying team. Get the team together early in the process.

- Doing research and asking questions may be embarrassing, time consuming, and tedious, but they are absolutely necessary to ensure that you make the right decision.

- Your funding resources must be equal to the business' financial demands. No amount of skill or commitment will make a business a success without the necessary working capital.

- A business is composed of many parts. Make sure you understand what each part represents and how it contributes to the success of the business.

- A business' financial statements provide the history of the business and insight into its current value and future growth. Go over the profit and loss statement, balance sheet, cash-flow analysis, and general ledger carefully with your professional advisers.

- Don't let your emotions lead you toward an investment that does not utilize your particular talents and experience. It can be fun, but it can also be dangerous.

- Consider a franchise only if it presents more of an opportunity than you could provide for yourself.

- When dealing with franchising, be wary of any franchise opportunity touting $1,000–3,000 starter kits. This may be too good to be true.

- Try to avoid pyramid schemes in franchising where you buy an area franchise and subfranchise to others.

- If you are not willing to play by the franchisor's rules, then don't buy a franchise. You would be better off to start your own business or buy an existing one.

- Have your attorney and accountant explain all the elements that constitute your relationship with the franchise company. You need to know your obligations and prerogatives.

- A good place to check out existing businesses and franchises is the Better Business Bureau. Make this step a part of your initial investigation.

Helpful Resources

Bond Franchise Guide
Source Book Publications
Oakland, CA
(510) 839-5462

This handy book contains information and data on hundreds of franchisors, as well as an overview of the franchise industry. Call for more information and how to order. $33.95.

Franchise Bible: How to Buy a Franchise or Franchise Your Own Business
The Oasis Press/PSI Research
Grants Pass, OR
(503) 479-9464
(800) 228-2275

If you are thinking of acquiring a franchise or franchising your own business, this indispensable guide will tell you how to do it and save you time and money in the process. Book includes sample documents and valuable resource materials. In addition, the book has been updated to cover the current and future franchising trends, including the new Uniform Franchise Offering Circular that was adopted by the FTC and the registration states, effective January 1, 1995. $19.95 for the paperback edition; $49.95 for the 2-volume, 3-ring binder edition.

Franchise Opportunities Handbook
U.S. Government Printing Office
Washington, DC 20402

The U.S. Department of Commerce annually compiles this publication which describes existing franchises in the country. The U.S. Government Printing Office prints and distributes it. Write to the above address for price and delivery options.

Franchisee Rights — A Self-Defense Manual for the Franchisee
Hammond & Morton
New York, NY
(212) 333-5353

This book is a handy resource for anyone considering a franchise. Call for more information.

Franchising: Regulation of Buying and Selling a Franchise
Bureau of National Affairs, Inc.
Rockville, MD
(800) 372-1033

A solid guide to the regulations involved in the buying and selling of a franchise.

International Franchise Association
1350 New York Avenue, NW, Suite 900
Washington, DC 20005

This association publishes miscellaneous titles on franchise topics. Write to the above address for a catalog. Although this association has voluntary membership, it is generally considered a good idea to check to see if the franchise you are considering is a member.

Pilot Books
103 Cooper Street
Babylon, NY 11702

This publisher has miscellaneous titles on franchise topics. Write for a catalog.

The Secrets to Buying and Selling a Business
The Oasis Press/PSI Research
Grants Pass, OR
(503) 479-9464
(800) 228-2275

The Secrets to Buying and Selling a Business (continued)

This helpful book will teach you the basic concepts involved in the purchasing process, but more importantly, it will help you recognize when a potential sale does not look good, saving you time and money. $19.95.

Starting and Operating a Business in ... **series**
The Oasis Press/PSI Research

Grants Pass, OR

(503) 479-9464
(800) 228-2275

This helpful series of books covers all 50 states, plus the District of Columbia. Updated annually, each book contains the latest state-specific and federal business information available. Learn about your state's taxes, laws, and the agencies created to help you start and operate your business more successfully! $24.95 for paperback or $29.95 for 3-ring binder.

Plan of Action for Buying a Business or Franchise

My company will be buying:
☐ An existing business ☐ A franchise

Use this planning tool to organize and prioritize the activities in this chapter that you need to do to start your business. Don't feel you have to list all the activities you have checked off. You can simply start with the top ten most important ones and go from there, or do whatever is easiest for you. Be sure to make plenty of copies of this cut-out worksheet for your planning and organizing activities for this chapter.

Action to be Taken	Begin Date	Who	Deadline

Plan of Action (continued)

Action to be Taken	Begin Date	Who	Deadline

Glossary

Accounts receivable financing. Accounts receivables represent the money owed to a business from credit sales to its customers. Next to cash, receivables are the most liquid of any firm's assets and they can be converted to cash within a short period of time. These qualities make receivables a desirable asset for any firm to hold, and for the same reason, often make desirable collateral for a loan.

Achievement tests. Achievement tests evaluate specific skills a person has attained through experience or education.

Affirmative action program. An affirmative action program is a plan for recruiting, hiring, training, and promoting minorities in industries where their numbers are low. Your business is probably not required to have such a program, unless you have certain federal government contracts.

Aptitude tests. Aptitude tests are mental tests that evaluate specific aptitudes like mechanical abilities, manual dexterity, or clerical abilities. Aptitude tests measure a person's ability to learn, not skills already learned.

Balance sheet. The balance sheet offers an overview of a firm's sources and amounts of financing, and how these funds have been used. This is an important document when making business decisions regarding financing.

Bond insurance. Bonds are a form of insurance that allow a third party to be guaranteed performance or compensated for nonperformance of a service a business or individual may perform. It is not uncommon for a bond to be required before someone will award you a contract. There are two types of bonds: 1) fidelity bonds are used to guarantee honest performance of employees; and 2) surety bonds are posted to guarantee the performance of a company.

Bulk sale law. When a business sells all or substantially all of its assets or enters into a major transaction that is not part of its ordinary business activities, the bulk sales law applies. The purpose of this law is to protect the rights of creditors, such as suppliers and others, who have advanced goods or money to a business and have not yet been paid; however, in recent years, these laws have been repealed in many states because of their complexity. Check to see if your state has repealed its bulk sale law.

Buying cycle. This is the time span from when a prospect becomes aware of a product or service to when he purchases it. Depending on the nature and cost of the product or service, the cycle could be days, weeks, or years.

Bylaws. The bylaws are the rules and procedures that govern a corporation. Such things as director and shareholder meetings and procedures are described in the bylaws. In the event of a conflict between the articles of incorporation and the bylaws, the articles control. Bylaws can't be inconsistent with a state's business corporation act.

Cash-flow projection. The cash-flow projection measures the cash impact of a firm's operating, investing, and financing activities over a given time period. This statement effectively combines balance sheet and income statement data to provide a summary of the sources of cash available to a business and how this cash was used. These variables are by far the most important indicators of a firm's financial health.

Cogeneration. Using the same fuel source to produce electricity and a useful heat energy at the same time is referred to as cogeneration.

Commercial bank. A commercial bank is a financial institution that obtains most of its working capital by accepting deposits from its customers. Depositors' funds are then used to conduct the bank's primary business of making loans and investments.

Commercial finance company. A commercial finance company is a lending institution that makes only secured short- and long-term loans to businesses. They offer no checking or savings account services. They are the business world's counterpart to consumer finance companies.

Cooperative or co-op advertising. Cooperative advertising is a method of sharing advertising costs with noncompetitive companies that target the same market as you do. It can help you generate more sales for less money.

Corporation. A corporation is a more complicated form of doing business because it is considered a distinct legal entity and has a legal status or existence separate from the owner or incorporator. One of the main advantages to incorporating is that you are not personally liable for corporation debts, as long as you comply with necessary corporate formalities. It is more expensive and complicated to incorporate and the help of an attorney is recommended.

Database (or relationship) marketing. Database marketing uses a database to specifically target and profile customers better, and it also penetrates the market through telemarketing or direct mail contacts. This type of marketing promotes regularly scheduled contacts and strong customer service. In other words, you develop strong relationships with customers so you can increase sales and reduce costs.

Daylighting. Daylighting uses the sun to light work areas via skylights and windows.

Debt financing. Debt financing represents the funds provided by creditors under a legally binding, contractual agreement. The contract obligates the borrower or debtor to repay the money or credit advanced, plus stipulated interest, at some designated future date, and to honor all other specified provisions or restrictions.

Demographics. The identification of common characteristics of a population — especially those of age, sex, income, and education — that allows you to determine to whom you should address your advertising message.

Due-diligence. This is proof or documentation that you have diligently inspected the property you are buying and found no environmental problems.

Employee handbook. An employee handbook includes your company's basic rules and regulations, usually only two to three pages in length. This is followed by information such as company history, procedures, benefits, and employee performance guidelines. Typically, an employee handbook is created from a company's policy and personnel manual, which consists of written policies and guidelines for both management and employees. In short, the employee handbook is a simplified version of the company's manual.

Equity financing. Equity financing is raised by selling a portion of a firm's ownership interest to an outsider of the business.

Executive summary. A business plan's executive summary gives the reader a chance to quickly understand your basic business concept. It helps the reader decide whether to commit more time to reading the entire plan.

Exit plan. Some investors, especially venture capitalists, plan to eventually liquidate their investment in your business by converting their holdings to cash or easily traded stock. Ideally, these investors want to know at the outset how they will get a substantial profit out of their investment. They want to see an exit plan included in your business plan.

Factoring company or house. A factoring company (or factor) pays cash for accounts receivables so that you can get use of your cash without waiting for 30,

60, or 90 days, depending on your credit terms. However, you will have to discount the receivables and may have to take back any bad accounts. Not all companies use factors, and factors may not take your accounts.

Fictitious business name. An assumed or fictitious business name is any name used in the course of business that does not include the full legal name of all the owners of the business. If your business goes by any name other than your own real name, your business is operating under a fictitious name.

Floor plan financing. Floor plan financing occurs when a retail operation sells large ticket items, such as appliances, trailers, boats, and cars. To finance each item's purchase, the bank will only charge interest payments on the item until it is sold. Once it is sold, then the retailer pays off the principal amount of the item.

Freight forwarder. A freight forwarder is an independent warehouser and shipper who handles domestic and international shipments for manufacturers who don't have the means to deliver everywhere they need to. The manufacturer pays the freight forwarder for this service.

Greywater. This is water that has already been used for nontoxic purposes, such as washing, food rinsing, or cooling.

Income statement. The income statement is a summary of the sales revenues earned in a given period and the expenses that were incurred in earning that revenue.

Independent contractor. An independent contractor is an individual who contracts her services out to a number of companies for compensation. This person is not considered an employee of the company, thus allowing the company to save on personnel paperwork and payroll taxes.

Joint and several liability. In a general partnership, joint and several liability makes any individual partner 100 percent responsible for any partnership obligation, regardless of whether that partner was solely or only partially responsible for the creation of the debt.

Leasing company. An independent leasing company provides your business with employees and takes care of all personnel functions from hiring to firing.

Limited liability company. A limited liability company (LLC) is not a corporation or partnership, yet it combines the corporate characteristic of limited liability for owners with partnership-type taxation. Advantages of selecting LLC status include pass-through tax treatment, limited liability, and active management participation. This form of doing business is available in the District of Columbia and in all 50 states, except for Hawaii, Massachusetts, and Vermont.

Line of credit. If you have seasonal or cyclical needs for cash, a line of credit may work for you. You may need to pay off the line for a 30-day period each twelve months, just to show that you don't need the loan for long-term financing. See what conditions your bank places on this type of borrowing.

Low-cost/no-cost measures. These are environment-friendly actions that require little expenditure to implement, such as providing reusable cups for your employees, or require no expenditure at all, such as reusing inter-office envelopes.

Management information system (MIS). An MIS is a systematic way of collecting, organizing, and distributing information to management in a summarized form to help them in planning, controlling, and making decisions about a company.

Market segment. A market segment is any group of consumers who have the same reaction to a given marketing stimulus. To be economically feasible, a market segment must be reachable through some means of communication, and it must be large enough to warrant a seller's effort.

Marketing plan. This plan outlines how to successfully penetrate, capture, and maintain desired positions in identified markets. In addition, it defines the goals, principles, and methods that determine a company's future. Refer to Chapter 3 for more details.

Media kits. A media kit is usually provided by a particular advertising medium and contains the kind of information you need to evaluate its advertising value. The media kit usually contains demographic and psychographic data of the medium audience, third-party circulation audits, and ad rates.

Media mix. Media mix is the combination of various communication instruments or channels — such as newspaper, video tape, magazines, or television — that effectively reach your target market. Using a combination of media can help you appear more credible and establish repetition of your message faster than using one medium alone.

Mission statement. A mission statement should concisely describe the goals, objectives, and underlying principles of your company. This statement can be placed at the beginning of the company description of your business plan to set the tone for your entire business plan, or it can be located near the end of that same section.

Narrative executive summary. A narrative executive summary is more like telling the reader a story; it can convey greater drama and excitement in presenting your business. It takes a capable writer to prepare a narrative summary that communicates the necessary information, engenders enthusiasm, and yet does not cross over the line into hyperbole.

News release. This document relates newsworthy information to a media source and should be written with the most vital information contained in the first paragraph. The first paragraph of a news release should answer the Five W's: who, what, where, when, and why.

Noncompetitive covenant. An agreement between the buyer and the seller, whereby the seller agrees not to compete with the buyer after the sale is complete.

Partnership. Any two or more individuals or entities who agree to contribute money, labor, property, or skill to a business and who agree to share in its profits, losses, and management are considered to have a partnership. A partnership can be organized in two different ways: as a general or as a limited partnership.

As a general partner, you have the right to share in management, but you have unlimited personal liability for the partnership's debts, taxes, and other obligations. As a limited partner, you have limited personal liability and are only liable for the amount of your investment in the partnership; however, the trade-off is that you must be a "silent partner" in the business and not have any say in its day-to-day operations.

Personality tests. Personality tests are either objective or subjective. The objective tests are usually computer-scored, yielding a personality profile. The subjective tests are those consisting of a person's response to or interpretation of ink blots, drawings, or photographs. The test-taker's verbal responses to the test are recorded and interpreted by a psychologist or psychiatrist.

Pro forma. This is a term used to designate future cash estimates for a business rather than using data from past experience. Therefore, a pro forma income statement is an estimate of income for the number of years you project into the future. By doing projections, you can anticipate when you will need cash and thus avoid running to the bank when you are in a financial crisis.

Psychographics. The lifestyle characteristics of a target market, such as hobbies, preferences, or social groups. These characteristics tell you what type of appeal may be most effective in reaching your prospect.

Representative or rep firms. Representative or rep firms are companies that contract with other companies to sell their products or services.

S corporation. An S corporation is a private corporation of 35 or fewer stockholders who pay personal income rather than corporate income tax on net profits. A corporation may elect to be treated as an S corporation under the Internal Revenue Code. Stringent rules exist with respect to how and when the election is made; the number and type of shareholders; and the means by which the election may be terminated.

Sales environment. The physical surroundings that set the stage so you can make your sales presentation as effectively as possible. A sales environment could be a retail location, client's office, or an outside meeting place, such as a restaurant.

Sales forecasting. This is the process of projecting your sales over a specific period of time.

Service mark. A service mark is the name used by a business to designate its service, such as Smith Legal Services or Smith Car Washes.

Sick building syndrome. This is the condition where building materials cause sickness or serious discomfort to employees.

Situational tests. Situational tests measure a person's ability to cope in realistic work settings, for instance, testing how quickly and accurately a person sorts 100 letters and places them in alphabetized office mailboxes.

Sole proprietorship. A sole proprietorship is a business that is owned by one person. Because there are no formal legal requirements for setting up a sole proprietorship, it is a relatively simple form to start and operate. A sole proprietor is personally liable for all business debts and must be aware of this risk and prepare for it. On the other hand, a sole proprietor can reap all the profits from the business.

Source reduction. Source reduction occurs when you reduce the amount of materials, or the quantity of a particular material, used to accomplish a specific task in your operations.

Spot. Most broadcast (television and radio) media buyers and salespeople refer to their advertisements or commercials as "spots."

Synopsis executive summary. A synopsis executive summary simply relates, in abbreviated fashion, the conclusion of each section of the completed business plan. Its advantage is that it is relatively easy to prepare and less dependent on a talented writer. The only disadvantage is that the tone of a "synopsis" summary tends to be rather dry.

Telemarketing. Telemarketing is a sales call that is made by phone. It can be used solely as an advertising method to generate interest and direct sales.

Temporary employment agencies. Temporary employment agencies specialize in "renting out" employees to fill a short-term need in a company for whatever length of time is required.

Test marketing. This is a small-scale introduction of a new product or service to test its attributes and salability. Test marketing results provide information on how the product or service must be refined to best suit the market's needs, thus providing a better opportunity for the product or service to succeed when it is finally "rolled out" on a full-scale basis.

Trade credit insurance. Trade credit insurance is probably most important where you depend on one or more companies to purchase most of your goods or services and where their nonpayment of an invoice would put you out of business.

Trademark. A trademark represents the brand name that designates a company's products, such as its car, food product, or invention. An example of a trademark would be Corvette, Fig Newton, or NordicTrack.

Trade name. A trade name designates a business, whether it is a sole proprietorship, partnership, or corporation. An example of a trade name would be Microsoft, Pepsi-Cola Company, or Nabisco.

Uniform franchise offering circular or FTC disclosure document. By law, the franchiser must provide this document to you: 1) at his first face-to-face personal meeting with you or the time for making disclosures regarding the terms and conditions of the sale of the franchise; 2) ten days before your making any payment to the franchiser; and 3) ten days before the signing of any contract committing you to buy the franchise, whichever occurs first.

Usury laws. Usury laws define the maximum amount of interest that may be charged on a credit transaction, such as a promissory note, that requires the payment of interest. Usury laws vary from state to state.

Venture capitalist. A venture capitalist is an individual or firm who invests money in new or expanding enterprises. They can be divided into two broad categories: those regulated by the federal government and those who are not. They are also characterized by the type of companies they invest in; the typical amounts they invest; and if they want to invest in start ups or ongoing businesses.

Vocational interest tests. Vocational interest tests reveal a person's likes and dislikes relative to general vocational or academic areas.

Wet garbage. This term is defined as anything organic, such as food scraps, vegetable trimmings, landscaping debris, or even pet waste. This also includes paper products and other nontoxic, biodegradable items.

Appendix B

Small Business Development Center State Directors' Offices

Small Business Development Centers (SBDCs) can be excellent sources of assistance and information. Besides being a helpful reference resource, SBDCs provide start-up information and sponsor business-oriented seminars. These centers, which are usually located on college and university campuses, are available in every state. To find the SBDC nearest you, contact your state's SBDC headquarters that is featured in this appendix. They will be able to refer you to the SBDC nearest you.

If you have a personal computer with a modem, you can find a list of your state's SBDCs by calling the U.S. Small Business Administration's electronic bulletin board system (BBS). The BBS provides a variety of other business-related information as well. This service is provided free and can be very handy and useful for the beginning business game player. Telecommunications settings are eight data bits, one stop bit, no parity. To log on to the system, dial:

SBA On-Line
(800) 697-4636

Another electronic bulletin board you can access that features a database for SBDCs is the Small Business Advancement Electronic Resource. For more information on this additional business resource, call:

Small Business Advancement Electronic Resource
(501) 450-5377

Alabama

Alabama SBDC Consortium
University of Alabama at Birmingham
Medical Towers Building
1717 11th Avenue, Suite 419
Birmingham, AL 35294-4410
(205) 934-7260
FAX (205) 934-7645

Alaska

Alaska SBDC
University of Alaska – Anchorage
430 West Seventh Avenue, Suite 110
Anchorage, AK 99501
(907) 274-7232
FAX (907) 274-9524

Arizona

Arizona SBDC Network
2411 West 14th Street, Suite 132
Tempe, AZ 85281
(602) 731-8720
FAX (602) 731-8729

Arkansas

Arkansas SBDC
University of Arkansas at Little Rock
100 South Main, Suite 401
Little Rock, AR 72201
(501) 324-9043
FAX (501) 324-9049

California

California SBDC Program
Department of Commerce
801 K Street, Suite 1700
Sacramento, CA 95814
(916) 324-5068
FAX (916) 322-5084

Colorado

Colorado SBDC
Colorado Office of Business Development
1625 Broadway, Suite 1710
Denver, CO 80202
(303) 892-3809
FAX (303) 892-3848

Connecticut

Connecticut SBDC
University of Connecticut
2 Bourn Place, U-94
Storrs, CT 06269-5094
(203) 486-4135
FAX (203) 486-1576

Delaware

Delaware SBDC
University of Delaware
Purnell Hall, Suite 005
Newark, DE 19716-2711
(302) 831-2747
FAX (302) 831-1423

District of Columbia

District of Columbia SBDC
Howard University
Sixth and Fairmont Streets NW, Room 128
Washington, DC 20059
(202) 806-1550
FAX (202) 806-1777

Florida

Florida SBDC Network
University of West Florida
19 West Garden Street, Suite 300
Pensacola, FL 32501
(904) 444-2060
FAX (904) 444-2070

Georgia

Georgia SBDC
University of Georgia
1180 East Broad Street
Athens, GA 30602-5412
(706) 542-5760
FAX (706) 542-6776

Hawaii

Hawaii SBDC Network
University of Hawaii at Hilo
200 West Kiwili
Hilo, HI 96720
(808) 933-3515
FAX (808) 933-3683

Idaho

Idaho SBDC
Boise State University
1910 University Drive
Boise, ID 83725
(208) 385-1640
FAX (208) 385-3877

Illinois

Illinois SBDC
Department of Commerce and
** Community Affairs**
620 East Adams Street, 6th Floor
Springfield, IL 62701
(217) 524-5856
FAX (217) 524-0171

Indiana

Indiana SBDC
Economic Development Council
One North Capitol, Suite 420
Indianapolis, IN 46204
(317) 264-6871
FAX (317) 264-3102

Iowa

Iowa SBDC
Iowa State University
137 Lynn Avenue
Ames, IA 50014
(515) 292-6351
FAX (515) 292-0020

Kansas

Kansas SBDC
Wichita State University
1845 Fairmount
Wichita, KS 67260-0148
(316) 689-3193
FAX (316) 689-3647

Kentucky

Kentucky SBDC
University of Kentucky
225 Business and Economics Building
Lexington, KY 40506-0034
(606) 257-7668
FAX (606) 323-1907

Louisiana

Louisiana SBDC
Northeast Louisiana University
700 University Avenue
Monroe, LA 71209-6435
(318) 342-5506
FAX (318) 342-5510

Maine

Maine SBDC
University of Southern Maine
96 Falmouth Street
Portland, ME 04103
(207) 780-4420
FAX (207) 780-4810

Maryland

Maryland SBDC
Department of Economic and
** Employment Development**
217 East Redwood Street, 10th Floor
Baltimore, MD 21202
(410) 333-6995
FAX (410) 333-4460

Massachusetts

Massachusetts SBDC
University of Massachusetts – Amherst
School of Management, Room 205
Amherst, MA 01003
(413) 545-6301
FAX (413) 545-1273

Michigan

Michigan SBDC
2727 Second Avenue
Detroit, MI 48201
(313) 964-1798
FAX (313) 964-3648

Minnesota

Minnesota SBDC
121 7th Place East, #500
St. Paul, MN 55101-2146
(612) 297-5770
FAX (612) 296-1290

Mississippi

Mississippi SBDC
University of Mississippi
Old Chemistry Building, Suite 216
University, MS 38677
(601) 232-5001
FAX (601) 232-5650

Missouri

Missouri SBDC
University of Missouri
300 University Place
Columbia, MO 65211
(314) 882-0344
FAX (314) 884-4297

Montana

Montana SBDC
Montana Department of Commerce
1424 Ninth Avenue
Helena, MT 59620
(406) 444-4780
FAX (406) 444-2808

Nebraska

Nebraska Business Development Center
University of Nebraska at Omaha
60th & Dodge Streets, CBA Room 407
Omaha, NE 68182
(402) 554-2521
FAX (402) 554-3747

Nevada

Nevada SBDC
University of Nevada – Reno
College of Business Administration – 032
Room 411
Reno, NV 89557-0100
(702) 784-1717
FAX (702) 784-4337

New Hampshire

New Hampshire SBDC
University of New Hampshire
108 McConnell Hall
Durham, NH 03824
(603) 862-2200
FAX (603) 862-4876

New Jersey

New Jersey SBDC
Rutgers University
180 University Avenue
Newark, NJ 07102
(201) 648-5950
FAX (201) 648-1110

New Mexico

New Mexico SBDC
Sante Fe Community College
P.O. Box 4187
Sante Fe, NM 87502-4187
(505) 438-1362
FAX (505) 438-1237

New York

New York State SBDC
State University of New York
SUNY Central Plaza, S-523
Albany, NY 12246
(518) 443-5398
FAX (518) 465-4992

North Carolina

North Carolina SBDC
University of North Carolina
4509 Creedmoor Road, Suite 201
Raleigh, NC 27612
(919) 571-4154
FAX (919) 571-4161

North Dakota

North Dakota SBDC
University of North Dakota
118 Gamble Hall, UND, Box 7308
Grand Fork, ND 58202
(701) 777-3700
FAX (701) 777-5099

Ohio

Ohio SBDC
77 South High Street
P.O. Box 1001
Columbus, OH 43266-0101
(614) 466-2711
FAX (614) 466-0829

Oklahoma

Oklahoma SBDC
Southeastern Oklahoma State University
P.O. Box 2584, Station A
Durant, OK 74701
(405) 924-0277
FAX (405) 920-7471

Oregon

Oregon SBDC
Lane Community College
44 West Broadway, Suite 501
Eugene, OR 97401-3201
(503) 726-2250
FAX (503) 345-6006

Pennsylvania

Pennsylvania SBDC
University of Pennsylvania
The Wharton School
444 Vance Hall, 3733 Spruce Street
Philadelphia, PA 19104-6374
(215) 898-1219
FAX (215) 573-2135

Rhode Island

Rhode Island SBDC
Bryant College
1150 Douglas Pike
Smithfield, RI 02917
(401) 232-6111
FAX (401) 232-6416

South Carolina

The Frank L. Roddey SBDC
University of South Carolina
College of Business Administration
Columbia, SC 29201-9980
(803) 777-4907
FAX (803) 777-4403

South Dakota

South Dakota SBDC
University of South Dakota
414 East Clark Street
Vermillion, SD 57069
(605) 677-5279
FAX (605) 677-5272

Tennessee

Tennessee SBDC
Memphis State University
Building 1, South Campus
Memphis, TN 38152
(901) 678-2500
FAX (901) 678-4072

Texas – Regional Offices

North Texas – Dallas SBDC
Bill J. Priest Institute for Economic Development
1402 Corinth Street
Dallas, TX 75215
(214) 565-5831
FAX (214) 565-5813

University of Houston SBDC
University of Houston
1100 Louisiana, Suite 500
Houston, TX 77002
(713) 752-8444
FAX (713) 756-1500

Northwest Texas SBDC
Texas Tech University
2579 South Loop 289, Suite 114
Lubbock, TX 79423
(806) 745-3973
FAX (806) 745-6207

UTSA South Texas Border SBDC
UTSA Downtown Center
1222 North Main Street, Suite 450
San Antonio, TX 78212
(210) 558-2450
FAX (210) 558-2464

Utah

Utah SBDC
University of Utah
102 West 500 South, Suite 315
Salt Lake City, UT 84101
(801) 581-7905
FAX (801) 581-7814

Vermont

Vermont SBDC
Vermont Technical College
P.O. Box 422
Randolph, VT 05060
(802) 728-9101
FAX (802) 728-3026

Virginia

Virginia SBDC
901 East Byrd Street, Suite 1800
Richmond, VA 23219
(804) 371-8253
FAX (804) 225-3384

Washington

Washington SBDC
Washington State University
Kruegel Hall, Suite 135
Pullman, WA 99164-4727
(509) 335-1576
FAX (509) 335-0949

West Virginia

West Virginia SBDC
950 Kanawha Boulevard, East
Charleston, WV 25301
(304) 558-2960
FAX (304) 558-0127

Wisconsin

Wisconsin SBDC
University of Wisconsin
432 North Lake Street, Room 423
Madison, WI 53706
(608) 263-7794
FAX (608) 262-3878

Wyoming

WSBDC/State Network Office
P.O. Box 3275
Laramie, WY 82071-3275
(307) 766-3505
FAX (307) 766-3406

Appendix C

National and State Business Magazines

One of the most vital aspects of operating a successful business is staying well informed on both national and state-specific trends and stories in areas such as business, industry, and technology. In addition, you will also want to stay abreast of upcoming legislation that may change how you do business or that may cost you more money in new taxes or labor requirements. By being on the cutting edge of new information, you can beat your competition in seizing a new market niche, securing the latest technological equipment, or grabbing a larger part of your target market. In short, your efforts of staying informed on national and local business-oriented news may mean increased sales or new opportunities for your business.

Reading national and state business magazines is one of the best ways to stay informed. National newspapers, such as *The Wall Street Journal*, and local newspapers are excellent sources. To familiarize you with some of the nation's prominent business magazines, and magazines specific to a particular state, this appendix features two listings of business magazines, respectively.

Review the listings at your convenience and consider subscribing to one or more of the publications. The phone numbers provided for each magazine will enable you to inquire about subscription information or to request more details about the publication's editorial content and special features.

National Business Magazines

ASBA Today
American Small Business Association
Grapevine, TX
(202) 628-6316

Bi-monthly publication edited for the ASBA and its members. Features articles on business, money, benefits, health, and grass roots information.

Business Start-Ups
Entrepreneur, Inc.
Irvine, CA
(714) 261-2325

Monthly publication that contains information on starting and running a business. Special emphasis on franchising and related business opportunities.

Business Week
Hightstown, NJ
(800) 635-1200 (Subscriber service)

A weekly magazine that features general business news, new products, and articles on a number of timely issues and topics affecting our nation's business, economy, and society.

Entrepreneur
Entrepreneur, Inc.
Irvine, CA
(714) 261-2325

Monthly publication that features information on running a small business. Contains management tips, entrepreneurial success stories, franchise information, and news and reviews of the latest in office equipment.

Entrepreneur's Digest
Oshkosh, WI
(414) 589-2900

Provides information on franchising, business opportunities, research, and start-up techniques tailored to business owners and professionals interested in becoming an entrepreneur. Published eight times per year.

Home Office Computing
Scholastic, Inc.
New York, NY
(212) 505-4220

Monthly publication edited for the home-based worker with news and information on getting the most from equipment. Features focus on new products and new ideas in time management, business practice, training, and telecomputing.

IB: Independent Business
Group IV Communications, Inc.
Thousand Oaks, CA
(805) 496-6156

Bi-monthly publication of the NFIB with focus on practical advice for the operation of a small business. Spotlight on company problems and procedures. Guide to management techniques and public relations. Also includes articles on governmental affairs affecting small business.

In Business
J.G. Press, Inc.
Emmaus, PA
(610) 967-4135

Bi-monthly publication edited for entrepreneurs who want to succeed in a business of their own. Articles focus on financing, tax planning, cash-flow management, staffing, and marketing. Departments include management tips, selling strategies, products and services that increase productivity, efficiency, and profitability.

Inc.
Boston, MA
(617) 248-8000 (Editorial)
(800) 234-0999 (Subscriptions)

Monthly publication that emphasizes the critical contribution of the small firm to the American economy. *Inc.* provides managers of small to mid-sized privately held companies with information on management approaches in finance, marketing, and personnel, as well as profiles of leading growth companies and analyses of economic and policy trends affecting the contemporary small growth firm.

Nation's Business
U.S. Chamber of Commerce
Washington, DC
(202) 463-5650 (*Nation's Business* magazine)
(202) 659-6000 (General information)

The U.S. Chamber of Commerce is interested in promoting and assisting small business around the country and its publication, *Nation's Business*, is a helpful source of emerging trends and issues facing small business.

Sales and Marketing Management
Bill Communications, Inc.
New York, NY
(212) 592-6200

A monthly magazine that provides helpful information on sales and marketing issues and trends that help business succeed. An annual *Survey of Buying Power* also provides comprehensive data on population, retail sales, and consumer-buying incomes for states, counties, and cities.

Small Business Opportunities
Harris Publications, Inc.
New York, NY
(212) 807-7100

A monthly magazine that offers practical advice to entrepreneurs, plus regular features on numerous franchise opportunities throughout the country. Would be a good source for researching franchise opportunities.

Spare Time
Kipen Publishing Corporation
Milwaukee, WI
(414) 543-8110

This magazine is for anyone interested in money-making opportunities, selling (full- or spare-time), starting a business, franchise openings, and profitable sidelines. Articles deal with home training programs, successful selling tips, and emphasizes individual success stories. Published nine times per year.

Your Company
American Express Publishing Corporation
(212) 522-1212

Quarterly publication sent at no charge to corporate cardmembers as a benefit of membership. Provides vital, concise, practical, and timely advice to small business owners seeking to better manage their companies. Offers financial insight, deal-closing strategies, legislative updates, news on the latest technology, and innovative management techniques.

State Business Magazines

Alabama

Business Alabama Monthly
P.O. Box 66200
Mobile, AL 36660
(205) 473-6269

Alaska

Alaska Business Monthly
P.O. Box 241288
Anchorage, AK 99524-1288
(907) 276-4373

Arizona

Arizona Business Magazine
3111 North Central, #230
Phoenix, AZ 85012
(602) 277-6045

Arkansas

Arkansas Business
210 East Markham, #200
Little Rock, AR 72201-1651
(501) 372-1443

California

Los Angeles Business Journal
5700 Wilshire Boulevard, Suite 170
Los Angeles, CA 90036
(213) 549-5225

Orange County Business Journal
4590 MacArthur Boulevard, Suite 100
Newport Beach, CA 92660
(714) 833-8373

(continued on next page)

California (continued)

Sacramento Business Journal
1401 21st Street, Suite 200
Sacramento, CA 95814
(916) 447-7661

Santa Clara Valley Business Journal
96 North Third Street, Suite 100
San Jose, CA 95112
(408) 295-3800

San Diego Business Journal
4909 Murphy Canyon Road, Suite 200
San Diego, CA 92123
(619) 277-6359

San Francisco Business Times
275 Battery Street, Suite 940
San Francisco, CA 94111
(415) 989-2522

Colorado

Colorado Business Magazine
7009 South Potomac Street
Englewood, CO 80112
(303) 397-7600

Connecticut

Business Times
315 Peck Street
New Haven, CT 06513
(203) 782-1420

Delaware

Delaware Business Review
240 North James Street, Suite 200A
Wilmington, DE 19804
(302) 998-9580

District of Columbia

Washington Business Journal
2000 14th Street, NW, Suite 500
Arlington, VA 22201
(202) 875-2200

Florida

Florida Trend
P.O. Box 611
St. Petersburg, FL 33731
(813) 821-5800

Georgia

Georgia Trend
1770 Indian Trail Road NW, Suite 350
Norcross, GA 30093
(404) 931-9410

National Small Business Journal
Atlanta, GA
(404) 605-0002

NSBJ is a unique business newspaper that
serves the Atlanta area. Provides high-quality,
how-to information, advice, and business tips
written by nationally prominent and locally
known experts and professionals. A free publication that is available at more than 600 locations.

Hawaii

Hawaii Business
825 Keeaumoku
P.O. Box 913
Honolulu, HI 96808
(808) 946-3978

Idaho

Idaho State Journal
305 South Arthur
P.O. Box 431
Pocatello, ID 83204
(208) 232-4161

Idaho Statesman
1200 North Curtis Road
P.O. Box 40
Boise, ID 83706
(208) 377-6200

The Idaho Business Review
4218 Emerald, Suite B
P.O. Box 7193
Boise, ID 83706
(208) 336-3768

Illinois

Chicago
414 North Orleans
Chicago, IL 60610-4418
(312) 222-8999

Crain's Chicago Business
740 North Rush Street
Winfield, IL 60611-2525
(312) 649-5411

Indiana

Business People
2410 Coliseum Boulevard North, Suite 100
Fort Wayne, IN 46805
(219) 426-0124

Iowa

Business Record
100 4th Street
Des Moines, IA 50309
(515) 288-3336

Kansas

Mid-America Commerce and Industry
1824 Cheyenne
Topeka, KS 66604
(913) 272-5280

Kentucky

Business Bulletin
464 Chenault Road
P.O. Box 817
Frankfort, KY 40602
(502) 695-4700

Business First
111 West Washington Street
P.O. Box 249
Louisville, KY 40202
(502) 583-1731

Kentucky Living
4515 Bishop Lane
P.O. Box 32170
Louisville, KY 40232
(502) 451-2430

Louisiana

Louisiana Municipal Review
P.O. Box 4327
Baton Rouge, LA 70821
(504) 344-5001

Maine

There is no listing for a state-specific
magazine in Maine.

Maryland

Warfield's Business Record
11 East Saratoga Street
Baltimore, MD 21202
(410) 752-1717

Massachusetts

Bay State Business Magazine
42 Thomas Patten Drive
Randolph, MA 02368-3902
(617) 961-2700

Boston Business
Boston Business Journal
200 High Street
Boston, MA 02110
(617) 330-1000

Business Magazine: South Shore
42 Thomas Patten Drive
Boston, MA 02368-3902
(617) 961-2700

New England Economic Review
Federal Reserve Building
P.O. Box 2076
Boston, MA 02106-2076
(617) 973-3403

Business Worcester
One Exchange Place
P.O. Box 300
Worcester, MA 01614-0300
(508) 799-0648

(continued on next page)

Massachusetts (continued)

Metronorth Business Review
199 Newbury Street
Danvers, MA 01923-1023
(508) 774-9434

Metrowest Business Review
Metrosouth Business Review
199 Newbury Street
Danvers, MA 01923-1023
(508) 774-9434

Michigan

Michigan Municipal Review
1675 Green Road
Ann Arbor, MI 48106
(313) 662-3246

The Business Consultant
Greater Detroit Chamber of Commerce
600 West Lafayette Boulevard
Detroit, MI 48226-3125
(313) 964-4000

Minnesota

Successful Business
18 1st Avenue, SE
Rochester, MN 55904
(507) 285-7600

Corporate Report – Minnesota
5500 Wayzata Boulevard, Suite 800
Minneapolis, MN 55416
(612) 591-2700

Mississippi

Mississippi Business Journal
P.O. Box 16445
Jackson, MS 39236-6445
(601) 352-9035

Missouri

Missouri Business
428 East Capitol
P.O. Box 149
Jefferson City, MO 65102
(314) 634-3511

Ingram's
306 East 12th Street, Suite 1014
Kansas City, MO 64106
(816) 842-9994

Montana

Montana Magazine
P.O. Box 5630
Helena, MT 59604
(406) 443-2842

Big Sky Business Journal
P.O. Box 3262
Billings, MT 59103
(406) 259-2309

Nebraska

Midlands Business Journal
11918 Poppleton Plaza
Omaha, NE 68144
(402) 330-1760

Nevada

Nevada Business Journal
2127 Paradise Road
Las Vegas, NV 89104
(702) 735-7003

New Hampshire

BNH: The Business of New Hampshire
404 Chestnut Street, Suite 201
Manchester, NH 03101
(603) 626-6354

New Hampshire Business Review
150 Dow Street
Manchester, NH 03101-1151
(603) 624-1442

New Jersey

New Jersey Business
New Jersey Business and Industry Association
310 Passaic Avenue
Fairfield, NJ 07006-2519
(201) 882-5004

New Mexico

New Mexico Business Journal
P.O. Box 30550
Albuquerque, NM 87190-0550
(505) 889-2911

New York

Crain's New York Business
220 East 42nd Street
New York, NY 10017-5846
(212) 210-0100

North Carolina

Business North Carolina
5435 Seventy-Seven Center Drive, Suite 50
Charlotte, NC 28217
(704) 523-6987

The Business Journal
128 South Tryon, Suite 2250
Charlotte, NC 28202-5003
(704) 347-2340

North Dakota

There is no listing for a state-specific
magazine in North Dakota.

Ohio

Ohio Magazine
62 East Broad Street
Columbus, OH 43215
(614) 461-5083

Oklahoma

Oklahoma Economic Development News
P.O. Box 26980
Oklahoma City, OK 73126
(405) 843-9770

Oklahoma Observer
P.O. Box 53371
Oklahoma City, OK 73152-3371
(405) 525-5582

Oregon

Oregon Business
921 SW Morrison, Suite 407
Portland, OR 97205
(800) 367-3466

*Oregon Business Opportunities &
Employment, Inc.*
895 Country Club Road, Suite C250
Eugene, OR 97401
(503) 484-1342

Pennsylvania

Central Penn Business Journal
409 South Second Street, Suite 3D
Harrisburg, PA 17104
(717) 236-4300

Eastern Pennsylvania Business Journal
5000 Tilghman Street, Suite 215
Allentown, PA 18104
(215) 398-1026

Northeast Pennsylvania Business Journal
3185 Lackawanna Avenue
Bloomsburg, PA 17815-3329
(717) 784-2121

Rhode Island

Providence Business News
300 Richmond Street, Suite 202
Providence, RI 02903
(401) 273-2201

Providence Journal
75 Fountain Street
Providence, RI 02902
(401) 277-7000

South Carolina

South Carolina Business Journal
1201 Main Street
Columbia, SC 29201-3200
(803) 799-4601

South Dakota

South Dakota Business Review
University of South Dakota
Business Research Bureau
School of Business
414 East Clark Street
Vermillion, SD 57069
(605) 677-5287

Tennessee

The Tennessee Magazine
710 Spence Lane
P.O. Box 100912
Nashville, TN 37224
(615) 367-9284

Texas

Austin Business Journal
1301 Capital of Texas Highway, C-200
Austin, TX 78746-6548
(512) 328-0180

Dallas Business Journal
4131 North Central Expressway, Suite 310
Dallas, TX 75204-3163
(214) 520-1010

Fort Worth Business Journal
501 Jones Street
Fort Worth, TX 76102
(817) 336-8300

Houston Business Journal
One West Loop South, Suite 650
Houston, TX 77027
(713) 688-8811

San Antonio Business Journal
3201 Cherry Ridge, #D-400
San Antonio, TX 78230-4823
(512) 341-3202

Utah

Utah Business
180 North Wright Brothers Drive, Suite 670
P.O. Box 22830
Salt Lake City, UT 84122-0830
(801) 328-8200

Vermont

New England Economic Review
Federal Reserve Building
P.O. Box 2076
Boston, MA 02106-2076
(617) 973-3403

Virginia

Virginia Business
411 East Franklin Street, #105
Richmond, VA 23219
(804) 649-8471

Virginia Town & City
P.O. Box 12164
Richmond, VA 23241
(804) 649-6999

Washington

Journal of Business
South 104 Division Street
Spokane, WA 99202
(509) 456-5257

West Virginia

The State Journal
904 Virginia Street West
Charleston, WV 25321
(304) 344-1630

Wisconsin

Corporate Report – Wisconsin
P.O. Box 870
Menomonee Falls, WI 53052
(414) 255-9077

Wisconsin Woman
207 East Buffalo Street, #419
Milwaukee, WI 53202-5712
(414) 273-1234

Wyoming

There is no listing for a state-specific
magazine for Wyoming.

Index

Marketing Mastery
Your Seven Step Guide

Every business needs to attract new customers – but at what cost? ***Marketing Mastery: Your Seven Step Guide to Success*** was written especially for small business owners and managers who want to know what works – and how to put it into use now. It's a practical, hands-on guide that will:

❏ Take you step-by-step from launching a new product to acquiring and keeping a core of satisfied-plus customers.

❏ Give you a comprehensive set of marketing tools and strategies, including the worksheets you need to develop a successful marketing plan.

Here's what people are saying about ***Marketing Mastery:***

"Better than dozens of similar books we've seen over the years... will help guarantee that your marketing plan succeeds."
The Denver Post

"Marketing Mastery *provides our members with a tool to map out their marketing plan, identify their target market, develop pricing formats, and identify many other marketing strategies. We feel this publication is an invaluable resource for small business."*

Bernie Thayer, President
National Association for the Self-Employed (NASE)

"A valuable tool for entrepreneurs who seek to develop a marketing plan that will work, complete with worksheets."
Leo R. Simpson, Ph.D.
Professor of Management
Eastern Washington University

Harriet Stephenson
and Dorothy Otterson

Co-authors Harriet Stephenson and Dorothy Otterson have worked with over 2,000 small business owners and trained hundreds of entrepreneurs and entrepreneurs-to-be in marketing skills and personal effectiveness. They've put the results of their experiences to work for you in...
Marketing Mastery: Your Seven Step Guide to Success.

Paperback $19.95	ISBN: 1-55571-357-2	**Pages: 240**
Binder $39.95	ISBN: 1-55571-358-0	**Pages: 240**

You can order directly from PSI/The Oasis Press:
300 North Valley Drive, Grants Pass, Oregon 97526
(503) 476-9464   FAX (503) 476-1479

Call toll free to order **Marketing Mastery: Your Seven Step Guide to Success**
1 - 8 0 0 - 2 2 8 - 2 2 7 5
All Major Credit Cards Accepted

BOOKS FROM THE OASIS PRESS® Please check the edition (binder or paperback) of your choice

TITLE	BINDER	PAPERBACK	QUANTITY	COST
The Business Environmental Handbook		☐ $ 19.95		
Business Owner's Guide to Accounting & Bookkeeping		☐ $ 19.95		
California Corporation Formation Package and Minute Book	☐ $ 39.95	☐ $ 29.95		
A Company Policy and Personnel Workbook	☐ $ 49.95	☐ $ 29.95		
Company Relocation Handbook	☐ $ 49.95	☐ $ 19.95		
Complete Book of Business Forms	☐ $ 49.95	☐ $ 19.95		
Controlling Your Company's Freight Costs	☐ $ 39.95			
Cost-Effective Market Analysis	☐ $ 39.95			
Debt Collection: Strategies for the Small Business	☐ $ 39.95	☐ $ 17.95		
The Essential Corporation Handbook		☐ $ 19.95		
Export Now	☐ $ 39.95	☐ $ 19.95		
Financial Management Techniques For Small Business	☐ $ 39.95	☐ $ 19.95		
Financing Your Small Business		☐ $ 19.95		
Franchise Bible: A Comprehensive Guide	☐ $ 49.95	☐ $ 19.95		
Home Business Made Easy		☐ $ 19.95		
How to Develop & Market Creative Business Ideas		☐ $ 14.95		
The Loan Package	☐ $ 39.95			
Mail Order Legal Guide	☐ $ 45.00	☐ $ 29.95		
Managing People: A Practical Guide	☐ $ 49.95	☐ $ 19.95		
Marketing Your Products and Services Successfully	☐ $ 39.95	☐ $ 18.95		
People Investment	☐ $ 39.95	☐ $ 19.95		
Power Marketing for Small Business	☐ $ 39.95	☐ $ 19.95		
Proposal Development: How to Respond and Win the Bid (HARDBACK BOOK)	☐ $ 39.95	☐ $ 19.95		
Retirement & Estate Planning Handbook	☐ $ 49.95	☐ $ 19.95		
Safety Law Compliance Manual for California Businesses		☐ $ 24.95		
Company Illness & Injury Prevention Program Binder (OR GET KIT WITH BOOK AND BINDER $49.95)	☐ $ 34.95	☐ $ 49.95		
Starting and Operating A Business in... BOOK INCLUDES FEDERAL SECTION PLUS ONE STATE SECTION —	☐ $ 29.95	☐ $ 21.95		
PLEASE SPECIFY WHICH STATE(S) YOU WANT				
STATE SECTION ONLY (BINDER NOT INCLUDED) — SPECIFY STATES	☐ $ 8.95	BOOK & BINDER KIT		
U.S. EDITION (FEDERAL SECTION — 50 STATES AND WASHINGTON, D.C. IN 11-BINDER SET)	☐ $295.00			
Successful Business Plan: Secrets & Strategies (GET THE BINDER...IT'S A BUSINESS PLAN KIT)	☐ $ 49.95	☐ $ 21.95		
Surviving and Prospering in a Business Partnership	☐ $ 39.95	☐ $ 19.95		
Write Your Own Business Contracts (HARDBACK BOOK)	☐ $ 39.95	☐ $ 19.95		

BOOK TOTAL (Please enter on other side also for grand total)

SOFTWARE Please check whether you use Macintosh or 5-1/4" or 3-1/2" Disk for IBM-PC & Compatibles

TITLE	5-1/4" IBM Disk	3-1/2" IBM Disk	MAC	PRICE	QUANTITY	COST
Business Planning System	☐	☐		☐ $129.95		
California Corporation Formation Package Software	☐	☐	☐	☐ $ 39.95		
★ California Corporation Formation Binderbook & Software	☐	☐	☐	☐ $ 69.95		
Company Policy & Personnel Software (Text Files)	☐	☐	☐	☐ $ 49.95		
★ Company Policy & Personnel Binderbook & Software (Text Files)	☐	☐	☐	☐ $ 89.95		
Customer Profile & Retrieval: Professional	☐	☐		☐ $119.95		
Financial Management Techniques		☐		☐ $ 99.95		
★ Financial Management Techniques Binderbook & Software		☐		☐ $129.95		
Financial Templates	☐	☐	☐	☐ $ 69.95		
The Small Business Expert	☐	☐		☐ $ 34.95		
Successful Business Plan (Full Standalone)	☐	☐		☐ $ 99.95		
★ Successful Business Plan Binderbook & Software (Full Standalone)	☐	☐		☐ $125.95		

SOFTWARE TOTAL (Please enter on other side also for grand total)

Please add above totals on other side to complete your order. Thanks!

PSI Successful Business Library / Tools for Business Success Order Form (please see other side also)
Call, Mail or Fax to: PSI Research, 300 North Valley Drive, Grants Pass, OR 97526 USA
Order Phone USA (800) 228-2275   Inquiries and International Orders (503) 479-9464   FAX (503) 476-1479

New titles coming to you from *The Oasis Press* in 1995.

Title	Pub.	Binder	Paperback	Quantity	Cost
A Firm Foundation: How To Secure Venture Capital	Sept.	☐ $ 39.95	☐ $ 19.95		
Comp Control: The Secrets of Reducing Workers' Compensation Costs	July	☐ $ 39.95	☐ $ 19.95		
Customer Engineering: Cutting Edge Selling Strategies	July	☐ $ 39.95	☐ $ 19.95		
Draw The Line: A Sexual Harassment Free Workplace	Sept.		☐ $ 17.95		
The Essential Limited Liability Company Handbook	July	☐ $ 39.95	☐ $ 19.95		
Funding for Women, Minorities and Disabled Entrepreneurs	Sept.	☐ $ 39.95	☐ $ 19.95		
Legal Expense Defense: How to Control Your Business' Legal Costs and Problems	July	☐ $ 39.95	☐ $ 19.95		
Successful Network Marketing for The 21st Century	June		☐ $ 14.95		

Place your order before publication date and get a 20% discount off of the regular price. Your credit card will not be billed until the day the book is shipped.

Sold to: PLEASE GIVE STREET ADDRESS NOT P.O. BOX FOR SHIPPING

Name _____   Title: _____

Company _____   Daytime Telephone: _____

Street Address _____

City/State/Zip _____

☐   *YES, I want to receive the PSI newsletter, MEMO.*
   Be sure to include: Name, address, and telephone number above.

Ship to: (if different) PLEASE GIVE STREET ADDRESS NOT P.O. BOX FOR SHIPPING

Name _____

Title _____

Company _____

Street Address _____

City/State/Zip _____

Daytime Telephone _____

Payment Information:

☐ Check enclosed payable to PSI Research (When you enclose a check, UPS ground shipping is free within the Continental U.S.A.)

Charge - ☐ VISA ☐ MASTERCARD ☐ AMEX ☐ DISCOVER   Card Number: _____ Expires ____

Signature: _____   Name on card: _____

EXECARDS — The Personal Business Communications Tool

ITEM	PRICE	QUANTITY	COST

TOTAL (Please enter also for grand total) $ _____

Many additional options available, including custom imprinting of your company's name, logo or message. Please request a complete catalog. 800-228-2275

Please send me:

_____EXECARDS Catalog

_____Oasis Press Software Information

_____Oasis Press Book Information

YOUR GRAND TOTAL

BOOK TOTAL (from other side) $ _____

BOOK TOTAL (1995 Titles) $ _____

SOFTWARE TOTAL (from other side) $ _____

EXECARDS TOTAL $ _____

TOTAL ORDER $ _____

Rush service is available. Please call us for details.

Use this form to register for advance notification of updates, new books and software releases, plus special customer discounts!

Please answer these questions to let us know how our products are working for you, and what we could do to serve you better.

Title of book or software purchased from us:_____

It is a:
- ☐ Binder book
- ☐ Paperback book
- ☐ Book/software combination
- ☐ Software only

Rate this product's overall quality of information:
- ☐ Excellent
- ☐ Good
- ☐ Fair
- ☐ Poor

Rate the quality of printed materials:
- ☐ Excellent
- ☐ Good
- ☐ Fair
- ☐ Poor

Rate the format:
- ☐ Excellent
- ☐ Good
- ☐ Fair
- ☐ Poor

Did the product provide what you needed?
- ☐ Yes ☐ No

If not, what should be added?_____
_____
_____
_____
_____
_____

This product is:
- ☐ Clear and easy to follow
- ☐ Too complicated
- ☐ Too elementary

Were the worksheets (if any) easy to use?
- ☐ Yes ☐ No ☐ N/A

Should we include:
- ☐ More worksheets
- ☐ Fewer worksheets
- ☐ No worksheets

How do you feel about the price?
- ☐ Lower than expected
- ☐ About right
- ☐ Too expensive

How many employees are in your company?
- ☐ Under 10 employees
- ☐ 10 – 50 employees
- ☐ 51 – 99 employees
- ☐ 100 – 250 employees
- ☐ Over 250 employees

How many people in the city your company is in?
- ☐ 50,000 – 100,000
- ☐ 100,000 – 500,000
- ☐ 500,000 – 1,000,000
- ☐ Over 1,000,000
- ☐ Rural (under 50,000)

What is your type of business?
- ☐ Retail
- ☐ Service
- ☐ Government
- ☐ Manufacturing
- ☐ Distributor
- ☐ Education

What types of products or services do you sell?
_____
_____
_____
_____

What is your position in the company?
(please check one)
- ☐ Owner
- ☐ Administration
- ☐ Sales/marketing
- ☐ Finance
- ☐ Human resources
- ☐ Production
- ☐ Operations
- ☐ Computer/MIS

How did you learn about this product?
- ☐ Recommended by a friend
- ☐ Used in a seminar or class
- ☐ Have used other PSI products
- ☐ Received a mailing
- ☐ Saw in bookstore
- ☐ Saw in library
- ☐ Saw review in:
  - ☐ Newspaper
  - ☐ Magazine
  - ☐ TV/Radio

Where did you buy this product?
- ☐ Catalog
- ☐ Bookstore
- ☐ Office supply
- ☐ Consultant
- ☐ Other_____

Would you purchase other business tools from us?
- ☐ Yes ☐ No

If so, which products interest you?
- ☐ EXECARDS® Communication Tools
- ☐ Books for business
- ☐ Software

Would you recommend this product to a friend?
- ☐ Yes ☐ No

If you'd like us to send associates or friends a catalog, just list names and addresses on back.

Do you use a personal computer for business?
- ☐ Yes ☐ No

If yes, which?
- ☐ IBM/compatible
- ☐ Macintosh

Check all the ways you use computers:
- ☐ Word processing
- ☐ Accounting
- ☐ Spreadsheet
- ☐ Inventory
- ☐ Order processing
- ☐ Design/graphics
- ☐ General data base
- ☐ Customer information
- ☐ Scheduling

May we call you to follow up on your comments?
- ☐ Yes ☐ No

May we add your name to our mailing list?

- ☐ Yes ☐ No

If there is anything you think we should do to improve this product, please describe: _____
_____
_____
_____

Thank you for your patience in answering the above questions.
Just fill in your name and address here, fold (see back) and mail.

Name _____
Title_____
Company _____
Phone_____
Address _____

If you have friends or associates who might appreciate receiving our catalogs, please list here. Thanks!

Name_____   Name_____

Title_____   Title_____

Company_____   Company_____

Phone_____   Phone_____

Address_____   Address_____

City/State/Zip_____   City/State/Zip_____

FOLD HERE FIRST

BUSINESS REPLY MAIL

FIRST CLASS MAIL PERMIT NO. 002 MERLIN, OREGON

POSTAGE WILL BE PAID BY ADDRESSEE

PSI Research
PO BOX 1414
Merlin OR 97532-9900

NO POSTAGE
NECESSARY
IF MAILED
IN THE
UNITED STATES

Please cut
along this
vertical line,
fold twice,
tape together
and mail.
Thanks!

Use this form to register for advance notification of updates, new books and software releases, plus special customer discounts!

Please answer these questions to let us know how our products are working for you, and what we could do to serve you better.

Title of book or software purchased from us:_____

It is a:
- ☐ Binder book
- ☐ Paperback book
- ☐ Book/software combination
- ☐ Software only

Rate this product's overall quality of information:
- ☐ Excellent
- ☐ Good
- ☐ Fair
- ☐ Poor

Rate the quality of printed materials:
- ☐ Excellent
- ☐ Good
- ☐ Fair
- ☐ Poor

Rate the format:
- ☐ Excellent
- ☐ Good
- ☐ Fair
- ☐ Poor

Did the product provide what you needed?
- ☐ Yes ☐ No

If not, what should be added?_____
_____
_____
_____
_____

This product is:
- ☐ Clear and easy to follow
- ☐ Too complicated
- ☐ Too elementary

Were the worksheets (if any) easy to use?
- ☐ Yes ☐ No ☐ N/A

Should we include:
- ☐ More worksheets
- ☐ Fewer worksheets
- ☐ No worksheets

How do you feel about the price?
- ☐ Lower than expected
- ☐ About right
- ☐ Too expensive

How many employees are in your company?
- ☐ Under 10 employees
- ☐ 10 – 50 employees
- ☐ 51 – 99 employees
- ☐ 100 – 250 employees
- ☐ Over 250 employees

How many people in the city your company is in?
- ☐ 50,000 – 100,000
- ☐ 100,000 – 500,000
- ☐ 500,000 – 1,000,000
- ☐ Over 1,000,000
- ☐ Rural (under 50,000)

What is your type of business?
- ☐ Retail
- ☐ Service
- ☐ Government
- ☐ Manufacturing
- ☐ Distributor
- ☐ Education

What types of products or services do you sell?
_____
_____
_____
_____

What is your position in the company?
(please check one)
- ☐ Owner
- ☐ Administration
- ☐ Sales/marketing
- ☐ Finance
- ☐ Human resources
- ☐ Production
- ☐ Operations
- ☐ Computer/MIS

How did you learn about this product?
- ☐ Recommended by a friend
- ☐ Used in a seminar or class
- ☐ Have used other PSI products
- ☐ Received a mailing
- ☐ Saw in bookstore
- ☐ Saw in library
- ☐ Saw review in:
  - ☐ Newspaper
  - ☐ Magazine
  - ☐ TV/Radio

Where did you buy this product?
- ☐ Catalog
- ☐ Bookstore
- ☐ Office supply
- ☐ Consultant
- ☐ Other_____

Would you purchase other business tools from us?
- ☐ Yes ☐ No

If so, which products interest you?
- ☐ EXECARDS® Communication Tools
- ☐ Books for business
- ☐ Software

Would you recommend this product to a friend?
- ☐ Yes ☐ No

If you'd like us to send associates or friends a catalog, just list names and addresses

**on back.
Do you use a personal computer for business?**
- ☐ Yes ☐ No

If yes, which?
- ☐ IBM/compatible
- ☐ Macintosh

Check all the ways you use computers:
- ☐ Word processing
- ☐ Accounting
- ☐ Spreadsheet
- ☐ Inventory
- ☐ Order processing
- ☐ Design/graphics
- ☐ General data base
- ☐ Customer information
- ☐ Scheduling

May we call you to follow up on your comments?
- ☐ Yes ☐ No

May we add your name to our mailing list?

☐ Yes ☐ No

If there is anything you think we should do to improve this product, please describe: _____
_____
_____
_____

**Thank you for your patience in answering the above questions.
Just fill in your name and address here, fold (see back) and mail.**

Name _____
Title_____
Company _____
Phone_____
Address _____

RR 2 4 4

If you have friends or associates who might appreciate receiving our catalogs, please list here. Thanks!

Name_____   Name_____

Title_____   Title_____

Company_____   Company_____

Phone_____   Phone_____

Address_____   Address_____

City/State/Zip_____   City/State/Zip_____

FOLD HERE FIRST

BUSINESS REPLY MAIL

FIRST CLASS MAIL PERMIT NO. 002 MERLIN, OREGON

POSTAGE WILL BE PAID BY ADDRESSEE

PSI Research
PO BOX 1414
Merlin OR 97532-9900

NO POSTAGE
NECESSARY
IF MAILED
IN THE
UNITED STATES

✂

Please cut
along this
vertical line,
fold twice,
tape together
and mail.
Thanks!